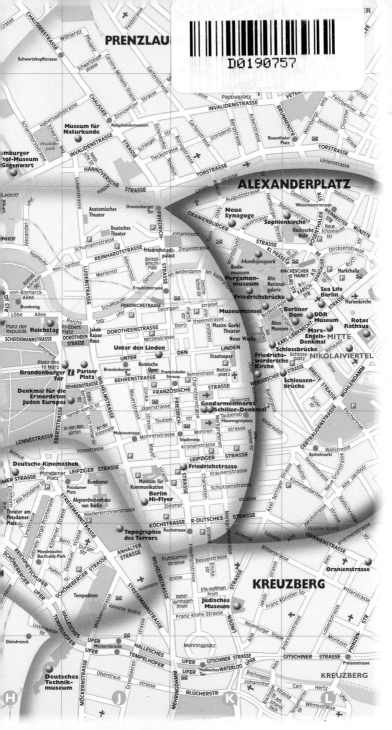

CITYPACK GUIDE TO
Berlin

How to Use This Book

KEY TO SYMBOLS

✚	Map reference to the accompanying fold-out map	🚢	Nearest riverboat or ferry stop
✉	Address	♿	Facilities for visitors with disabilities
☎	Telephone number	❓	Other practical information
🕓	Opening/closing times	▷	Further information
🍴	Restaurant or café	ℹ	Tourist information
🚉	Nearest rail station	✋	Admission charges: Expensive (more than €8) Moderate (€4–€8) Inexpensive (€4 or less)
Ⓜ	Nearest subway (Metro) station		
🚌	Nearest bus route		

This guide is divided into four sections

• Essential Berlin: An introduction to the city and tips on making the most of your stay.

• Berlin by Area: We've broken the city into eight areas, and recommended the best sights, shops, entertainment venues, nightlife and restaurants in each one. Suggested walks help you to explore on foot.

• Where to Stay: The best hotels, whether you're looking for luxury, budget or something in between.

• Need to Know: The info you need to make your trip run smoothly, including getting about by public transport, weather tips, emergency phone numbers and useful websites.

Navigation In the Berlin by Area chapter, we've given each area of the city its own color, which is also used on the locator maps throughout the book and the map on the inside front cover.

Maps The fold-out map accompanying this book is a comprehensive street plan of Berlin. The grid on this fold-out map is the same as the grid on the locator maps within the book. We've given grid references within the book for each sight and listing.

Contents

Introducing Berlin

Berlin has certainly lived through interesting times. Ascents, decline, fall and rise again followed each other in rapid succession through the 20th century. That's all history now. Berlin is back on the map and moving forward in the 21st century.

What is Berlin? The city is not easy to describe in words; it's the capital of a reunified federal Germany, but that reveals little. A place of baleful recollection and courageous defiance, all in living memory, but that doesn't tell you about right now. A vast studio for artists and a building site for entrepreneurs and government departments—that says more.

Berlin is a walk through the green hectares of the Grunewald and the Tiergarten, and a constricted stroll around the grim obstacle course of the Holocaust Memorial. It is a café terrace on the banks of the Spree and a Turkish coffee house in Kreuzberg; a designer shopping expedition on Ku'damm and a stroll around the New Age shops in Prenzlauer Berg; a night at the Deutsche Oper and an ear-splitting rave at the repurposed brewery now dubbed the KulturBrauerei. Berlin can be both *gemütlich* and hard-edged, sardonic and sentimental, cultivated and raucous, multi-cultural and narrow-minded. In a sense this city is still divided into East and West, this time by an invisible yet slowly fading line in its psyche.

Alternative lifestyles abound. Cabaret is going strong, and transvestite shows are legion. Visitors pour in for the Christopher Street Day gay and lesbian festival or the *Karneval der Kulturen,* as well as for business conventions. An exuberant feeling of something new abounds, an energy that needs to find an outlet, and Berlin has plenty of those.

Above all, Berlin is once again where it was destined to be: one of the great European capitals, warts and all.

Facts + Figures

- **The population of Berlin is 3.5 million.**
- **49 percent of the population is male; 51 percent female.**
- **14 percent are foreign nationals; 12 percent of citizens are of foreign/ethnic minority, a third of them Turkish.**

HEART TRANSPLANT

A new city heart has emerged between Potsdamer Platz and the government district along the former east–west border. Completely destroyed during World War II, this area was the biggest building site in Europe during the 1990s. Today, it is a bustling entertainment and business district, reflecting Berlin's modern architectural face.

THE CÖLLN WALL?

Medieval Cölln, on the River Spree's south bank, was founded in 1237, seven years before Berlin on the north bank. The two sister towns developed side by side until 1710, when Cölln was subsumed into Berlin. If it had gone the other way, which could so easily have happened, Germany's capital would be known today as Cölln (but probably spelled Kölln).

FRESH AIR

Nearly a third of Berlin consists of parks, meadows, woodland, lakes (Berlin is surrounded by lakes) and rivers. There are more than 16,000ha (39,500 acres) of woodland inside the city. Parks, castle grounds, zoos and botanical gardens all provide spaces to relax in and keep the city air relatively clean.

A Short Stay in Berlin

DAY 1

Morning Start the day with a stroll through the **Tiergarten** (▷ 66–67). Aim to end at the **Brandenburger Tor** (▷ 60), from where you can easily reach the **Reichstag** (▷ 65), where the federal German parliament sits.

Mid-morning Go south, taking in the grim spectacle of the **Denkmal für die Ermordeten Juden Europas** (▷ 69) along the way, to monumental **Potsdamer Platz** (▷ 39–48). From here it's not far along Potsdamer Strasse to the **Gemäldegalerie** (▷ 42–43) for a session of serious art appreciation.

Lunch To be kind to your feet at this point, go up onto Tiergarten Strasse and take bus 200 west to Breitscheidplatz. Then cross over to **Kurfürstendamm** (▷ 33). For a light lunch, choose either **Soupkultur** (▷ 38), or one of the great snack bars inside **KaDeWe** (▷ 36).

Afternoon Backtrack the short distance to Breitscheidplatz for a close-up look at the bomb-blasted **Kaiser-Wilhelm-Gedächtniskirche** (▷ 32), and pass a few moments in quiet contemplation in its memorial chapel.

Mid-afternoon Either walk via side streets, or take bus M45 northwest to Luisenplatz. From here you can visit ornate **Schloss Charlottenburg** (▷ 24–25). Before doing so, look in at the **Keramik-Museum** (▷ 26).

Dinner Multiple public transport options can take you all the way to Mitte at **Unter den Linden** (▷ 68). German dining should be on your agenda for the first day; **Dressler** (▷ 72) is a good mid-range choice.

Evening For culture try the **Deutsche Oper** (▷ 27) or the **Konzerthaus** (▷ 71), or for some alternative theater the **Maxim Gorki Theater** (▷ 71).

Morning Start out at the corner of **Friedrichstrasse** (▷ 61) and Kochstrasse to take in that Cold War-era Berlin Wall sight, Checkpoint Charlie. Head up Friedrichstrasse, and pop into French-owned department store **Galeries Lafayette** (▷ 70) on the way. At Unter den Linden turn right. Next to the **Staatsoper** (▷ 71) is the **Opernpalais Unter den Linden** (▷ 72), a café where you can have a coffee or breakfast.

Mid-morning Cross the River Spree to **Museumsinsel** (▷ 78–79), thickly clustered with stellar museums to choose from.

Lunch You can go to one of the museum cafés for lunch; leave Museumsinsel and take in some American diner munchies on the far side of **Monbijou Park** (▷ 82), at **Sixties** (▷ 86).

Afternoon Stroll around some of the alternative galleries in and around the **Hackesche Höfe** (▷ 84, 85), before crossing Karl-Liebknecht-Strasse to the **Marx-Engels-Denkmal** memorial (▷ 82) to wonder what the founders of Communism would have made of it all.

Mid-afternoon Take some time to explore **Alexanderplatz** (▷ 73—86), the heart of the old East Berlin. Take the elevator to the top of the Fernsehturm for an unparalleled view over the city.

Dinner Take the U-Bahn two stops to Senefelderplatz and walk the short distance to **Kollwitzplatz** (▷ 91) and adjacent Wörther Strasse, to dine at the great Thai restaurant **Mao Thai Stammhaus** (▷ 94).

Evening Since you are now in trendy Prenzlauer Berg, why not take in some dance and music action at the **Kesselhaus** (▷ 93).

ESSENTIAL BERLIN TOP 25

▶ ▶ ▶

Alexanderplatz ▷ 76
This historic square has been transformed into a bustling meeting place.

Bauhaus-Archiv ▷ 44
Simplicity and functionalism are expressed by the Bauhaus school of design.

Bergmannstrasse ▷ 52
This major street encompasses the multiethnic face of the Kreuzberg district.

Zoo Berlin ▷ 34 One of the world's most important zoos, with outdoor enclosures creating a sense of openness.

Unter den Linden ▷ 68
Fine buildings and superb statues in the former heart of imperial Berlin.

Tiergarten ▷ 66–67
A peaceful haven in the heart of the city with ornamental gardens, lakes and wooded areas to explore.

Spandauer Zitadelle ▷ 100 An attractive suburb with an ancient fortress on the rivers Havel and Spree.

Schloss Charlottenburg ▷ 24–25 Explore this lavish royal palace and its riverside grounds, just minutes from central Berlin.

Reichstag ▷ 65 Visit the spectacular glass dome of the German parliament building.

Pergamonmuseum ▷ 81
Houses the city's impressive collection of archaeological discoveries.

Pariser Platz ▷ 64
A handsome monumental square that's at the heart of Berlin.

Oranienstrasse ▷ 53
Buzzing with life, this long street is the soul of "alternative" Kreuzberg.

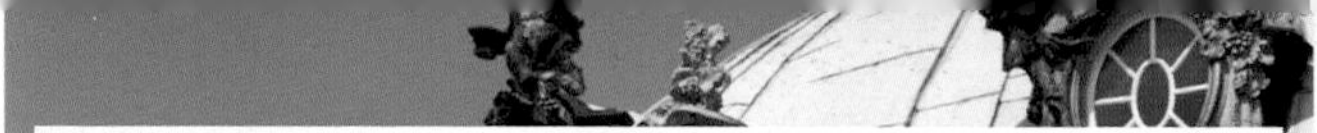

These pages are a quick guide to the Top 25, which are described in more detail later. Here they are listed alphabetically and the tinted background shows which area they are in.

Berliner Dom ▷ 77 The highly decorated dome of Berlin's Protestant cathedral is accessible to the public.

Brandenburger Tor ▷ 60 The city's last remaining city gate is Berlin's most symbolic landmark.

Ethnologisches Museum ▷ 98 The collection has displays from Oceania, the Americas and more.

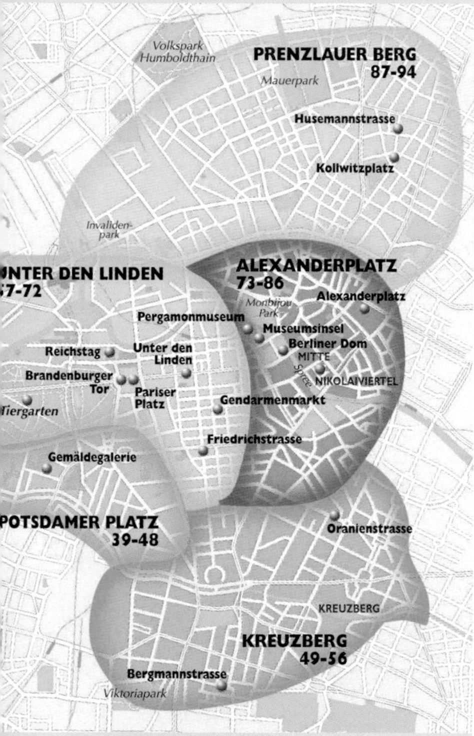

Volkspark Humboldthain
PRENZLAUER BERG 87-94
Mauerpark
Husemannstrasse
Kollwitzplatz
Invaliden-park
ALEXANDERPLATZ 73-86
NTER DEN LINDEN
7-72
Monbijou Park
Alexanderplatz
Pergamonmuseum
Museumsinsel
Berliner Dom
MITTE
Spree
NIKOLAIVIERTEL
Reichstag
Unter den Linden
Brandenburger Tor
Pariser Platz
Tiergarten
Gendarmenmarkt
Friedrichstrasse
Gemäldegalerie
POTSDAMER PLATZ 39-48
Oranienstrasse
KREUZBERG
KREUZBERG 49-56
Bergmannstrasse
Viktoriapark

Friedrichstrasse ▷ 61 This shopping street is also home to theaters, restaurants and bars.

Gemäldegalerie ▷ 42–43 This modern gallery holds some 2,700 European paintings.

Gendarmenmarkt ▷ 62–63 This lovely square is bounded by a museum, a theater and two cathedrals.

Husemannstrasse ▷ 90 This is a newly hip area, along with Kollwitzplatz.

Jagdschloss Grunewald ▷ 99 This hunting lodge, now a museum, is situated in a forest west of the city.

Kaiser-Wilhelm-Gedächtniskirche ▷ 32 These stark ruins are a monument to the horrors of war.

Kollwitzplatz ▷ 91 Around this street, Prenzlauer Berg is humming with life and energy.

Nikolaiviertel ▷ 80 An old quarter with cobbled streets and arcades lined with craft and gift shops.

Museumsinsel ▷ 78–79 Museum Island is home to some of Berlin's finest museums.

Kurfürstendamm ▷ 33 The bustling Ku'damm has a diverse array of shops and entertainment venues.

Shopping

Berlin has plenty to offer shoppers and the city is increasingly trading on its consumer appeal to attract visitors. You can buy everything here from designer labels and luxury jewelry to chic furniture and unusual gifts.

Retail Therapy

Brand shoppers and designer-label fans will be at home among names such as Gucci, Cerruti, Yamamoto and Diesel on Friedrichstrasse. Kurfürstendamm in the west of the city also has its fair share of the big names, including Versace and Gaultier. There are more than a dozen department stores in the city catering to all tastes and trends. The opulent KaDeWe (Kaufhaus des Westens), just off Ku'damm, with a seemingly inexhaustible array of merchandise on six floors, is the largest. Galeries Lafayette, off Friedrichstrasse, has a fantastic food hall in the basement and the Arkaden in Potsdamer Platz has a wide selection of top brands on three floors, with restaurants and cafés on the top floor for relaxing and refueling.

Individual Style

For something a little less mainstream you might want to head for the weird and wonderful shops around Oranienburger Strasse in Mitte, Bergmannstrasse and Oranienstrasse in Kreuzberg and Goltzstrasse in Schöneberg for bizarre shoes and bags, crazy clothes and trendy shades and jewelry. Off the beaten track, spend an afternoon window-shopping or picking up some unusual items in some of the offbeat shops around Kreuzberg and Prenzlauer Berg. Kastanienallee in Prenzlauer Berg is the

SECONDHAND

Trendsetters in this style-conscious capital are not afraid to celebrate the past. There are many retro and alternative clothing outlets around Prenzlauer Berg, but if you are serious about secondhand shopping head for the larger outlets such as Kleidermarkt (▷ 47), where you buy clothing by the kilo.

From confectionery and sausages to designer fashion and souvenirs, Berlin sells it all

heart of Berlin's alternative fashion scene, where you will find funky accessories, gifts and quirky up-and-coming designer boutiques. The city has a vibrant art scene, attracting dealers and collectors from all over the world; some of the most interesting art galleries are clustered around Auguststrasse in Mitte.

East and West

There are plenty of shops selling GDR memorabilia and clothing. A daily market in Alexanderplatz sells genuine army uniforms and badges; shops around Hackescher Markt and Prenzlauer Berg sell retro and cult clothing, accessories and souvenirs paying tribute to the city's history. Look out for souvenirs and clothing bearing the Ampelmann logo, the green-and-red-hat-wearing man seen at stop signs in the former east of the city. Other unique purchases include homemade chocolates, delicious breads and fine royal porcelain, both recent and antique items, made by KPM.

Malls

On days when the weather is simply too bad to be out on the street shopping, head for one of the big malls instead. For mainstream shopping, the Europa-Center on Tauentzienstrasse, the Uhlandpassage and the Kempinski Plaza on Uhlandstrasse, are all central and have plenty of choice. Out east there's the Berliner Markthalle on Rosa-Luxemburg-Strasse.

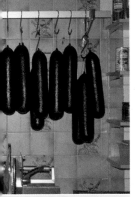

Beer tankards (top); designer gear in a chic store (middle); puppets in a toy shop (bottom)

MARKETS

Berlin has a huge number of flea markets selling clothing, jewelry and antiques. For surprising finds head for the antiques market (Wed–Mon) on Georgenstrasse under the S-Bahn arches. You can pick up some exotic bargains at the Turkish Market on Kollwitzplatz on Thursday afternoons. Weekly street markets are a great place to experience the multicultural tastes of the city. The Winterfeldtplatz market on Wednesday and Saturday morning is the best. Mingle among the friendly crowd and sample some Turkish, Italian and Greek delicacies.

Shopping by Theme

Whether you're looking for a department store, a quirky boutique, or something in between, you'll find it all in Berlin. On this page shops are listed by theme. For a more detailed write-up, see the individual listings in Berlin by Area.

BOUTIQUES AND DESIGNER CLOTHES

BagAge (▷ 55)
Bergmann (▷ 55)
Bip Boutique Barbara Neubauer (▷ 36)
Bleibgrün (▷ 36)
Chapeaux Hutmode Berlin (▷ 36)
Diesel (▷ 36)
Eisdieler (▷ 93)
Nix (▷ 85)
Respectmen (▷ 85)
Stoffwechsel (▷ 85)

DEPARTMENT STORES AND MALLS

Friedrichstadt-Passagen Q205 (▷ 70)
Galeries Lafayette (▷ 70)
KaDeWe (Kaufhaus des Westens) (▷ 36)
Potsdamer Platz Arkaden (▷ 47)

GALLERIES

Gipsformerei (▷ 27)
Hackesche Höfe (▷ 85)
Villa Grisebach (▷ 36)

THE HOME

Art & Industry (▷ 36)
Bella Casa (▷ 55)
Dom (▷ 70)
Guru-Laden (▷ 93)
Jean et Lili (▷ 93)
KPM (▷ 36)
Rosenthal (▷ 36)

MARKETS AND FOOD SHOPS

Berliner Antik und Flohmarkt (▷ 70)
Berliner Kaffeerösterei (▷ 36)
Berliner Kunst-und-Nostalgie-Markt (▷ 70)
Fassbender & Rausch (▷ 70)
Königsberger Marzipan Wald (▷ 27)

Trödelmarkt am Rathaus Schöneberg (▷ 47)
Trödelmarkt Strasse des 17. Juni (▷ 36)
Türkischer Markt (▷ 55)
Winterfeldtmarkt (▷ 36)

SECONDHAND AND OFFBEAT

Kleidermarkt (▷ 47)
Mr & Mrs Peppers (▷ 93)
Schallplatten Franz & Josef (▷ 93)
Sterling Gold (▷ 85)
VEB Orange (▷ 93)

SOUVENIRS

Berle's Trends and Gifts (▷ 70)
Erzgebirgskunst Original (▷ 85)

THE BEST OF THE REST

Belladonna (▷ 55)
Berliner Zinnfiguren (▷ 36)
Books in Berlin (▷ 27)
Bürgelhaus (▷ 70)
Dussmann (▷ 70)
Harry Lehmann (▷ 27)
Haus am Checkpoint Charlie (▷ 70)
Marga Schoeller Bücherstube (▷ 36)
Meissener Porzellan (▷ 70)
Sony Style Store (▷ 47)

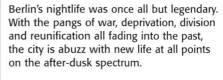

Berlin by Night

Berlin's nightlife was once all but legendary. With the pangs of war, deprivation, division and reunification all fading into the past, the city is abuzz with new life at all points on the after-dusk spectrum.

24-Hour Party
Nightlife continues well into the morning in Berlin as there are no licensing hours restrictions on opening times. Things don't really get going until after midnight, but the latest place to meet before the party starts is the after-work club, where lounges encourage you to wind down and relax before you hit the town.

Clubs
Berlin's club scene is split into two categories: institutions that have stood the test of time and single-occasion parties playing the latest sounds publicized via word of mouth within the extremely prolific underground scene. Established clubs are probably the best bet, and there is plenty of choice, but you should check out the latest listings as most have diverse offerings and events on certain nights may not be to your taste.

Performance
The cultural scene in Berlin ranges from traditional opera houses and cabarets to experimental theater, live jazz and new metal bands, with something to cater to all tastes. Due to its four decades-long division into East and West, the city now has two of some major cultural venues.

By night Berlin is an illuminated wonder of modern and Romanesque architecture

LISTINGS

Useful listings magazines include *Prinz, Tip, Zitty* (all twice-monthly, in German); *Berlin Das Magazin* (quarterly, in English and German); *Berlin Programm* (monthly, in German). *Prinz* also publishes an annual magazine picking out the best restaurants, shops, bars, clubs and hotels. Berlin Tourismus Marketing publishes *Berlin-Kalendar* every two months in English and German. Online, www.berlinatnight.de is informative.

Eating Out

Sure, Berlin is a great place for trying all kinds of traditional, regional German cuisine. But increasing cosmopolitanism, wealth and confidence has spawned a wave of new and varied dining experiences to suit all palates.

Breakfast and Snacks
Bakeries (*Bäckereien*) serve an array of pastries, cakes and coffees, and sometimes rolls and sandwiches. Many bakeries also have a small seating or standing area for "eating in." Snack bars (*Imbissstuben*) usually serve a few varieties of sausage in a bread roll, and may also offer fries, burgers and kebabs. Most have a standing area. Cafés often open as early as 7am, and tend to serve light snacks and hot and cold fast food, in addition to *Kaffee und Kuchen* (coffee and cake).

Traditional Fare
Plates come piled high with the two local staples, meat (usually pork) and potatoes, often accompanied by sauerkraut (pickled cabbage), peas and pickle. *Buletten* (meatballs) and *Kartoffelpuiffer* (potato pancakes) are Berlin specialties. Young Germans are eschewing this diet and an increasing number of restaurants reflect the modern taste for lighter fare. Beer halls (*Brauhäuser*) are the places to try traditional food and sample the local beer, which is generally brewed on the premises. Vegetarians should look for the words *"vegetarische Gerichte"* (vegetarian dishes) on the menu. In beer halls it's difficult to find a dish that doesn't include meat or meat stock.

From street cafés to sophisticated restaurants, Berlin offers a plethora of dining experiences

---

SMOKING BAN

In January 2008 a smoking ban was introduced in Berlin along the lines of ones in place in other EU countries and in New York. Smoking is forbidden in restaurants, bars, pubs and clubs, unless a dedicated smoking room is provided; anyone breaking the law faces a fine of up to €100. The law has proved unpopular, maybe as Germany has one of the highest smoking rates in the world.

Restaurants by Cuisine

There are restaurants to suit all tastes and budgets in Berlin. On this page they are listed by cuisine. For a more detailed description of each restaurant, see Berlin by Area.

AMERICAN

Sixties (▷ 86)

ASIAN

Golden Buddha (▷ 94)
Good Friends (▷ 28)
Mao Thai Stammhaus
  (▷ 94)
Mirchi (▷ 86)
Monsieur Vuong (▷ 86)
Sumo (▷ 56)
Tokyo Haus (▷ 28)

AUSTRALIAN

Corroboree (▷ 48)

AUSTRIAN

Diener Tattersaal (▷ 38)

CAFÉS

Café Aedes-West (▷ 38)
Café Bravo (▷ 86)
Café Einstein (▷ 72)
Café Einstein Stammhaus
  (▷ 48)

Café Übersee (▷ 56)
Café am Ufer (▷ 56)
Caffè e Gelato (▷ 48)
Opernpalais Unter den-
  Linden (▷ 72)
Soupkultur (▷ 38)
Zum Nussbaum (▷ 86)

FRENCH

Alt-Luxemburg (▷ 28)
Borchardt (▷ 72)
Lorenz Adlon (▷ 72)

GERMAN

Bergmann Curry (▷ 56)
Dressler (▷ 72)
Gambrinus (▷ 86)
Henne (▷ 56)
Kaisersaal (▷ 48)
Kartoffelkiste (▷ 38)
Knese (▷ 38)
Konnopke's Imbiss
  (▷ 94)
Luisen-Bräu (▷ 28)
Marjellchen (▷ 38)
Metzer Eck (▷ 94)
Neugrüns Köche (▷ 94)
Schnitzelei (▷ 28)
Vau (▷ 72)
Weinstein (▷ 94)

INDIAN

Amrit (▷ 56)
Paras (▷ 28)

ITALIAN

Ana e Bruno (▷ 28)
Bocca di Bacco (▷ 72)
Casolare (▷ 56)
Ossena (▷ 86)

Oxymoron (▷ 86)
Trattoria Piazza Rossa
  (▷ 86)
Vapiano (▷ 48)
Die Zwölf Apostel
  (▷ 72)

MIDDLE EASTERN

Sufissimo (▷ 56)

MIXED EUROPEAN

Ellipse Lounge (▷ 48)
Facil (▷ 48)
Frannz (▷ 94)
Funkturm Restaurant
  (▷ 28)
Hackescher Hof (▷ 86)
Hugos (▷ 38)
Julius (▷ 48)
Lutter & Wegner
  (▷ 30, 72)
Margaux (▷ 72)
Wintergarten im
  Literaturhaus (▷ 38)

MEXICAN

Frida Kaho (▷ 94)

PACIFIC

Vox (▷ 48)

RUSSIAN

Pasternak (▷ 94)

TURKISH

Hasir (▷ 56)
Istanbul (▷ 28)

Top Tips For...

However you'd like to spend your time in Berlin, these top suggestions should help you tailor your ideal visit. Each sight or listing has a fuller write-up elsewhere in the book.

CHIC SHOPPING

Bleibgrün (▷ 36): If it's good enough for Paris…
KaDeWe (▷ 36): For the best of just about everything.
Fassbender & Rausch (▷ 70): The chocolates here really are wicked.

UN-CHIC SHOPPING

Berliner Zinnfiguren (▷ 36): Military miniatures for the serious enthusiast.
Books in Berlin (▷ 27): All kinds of books in English and German.
Türkischer Markt (▷ 55): The edible side of Turkish Kreuzberg.

Berliners like to keep ahead of fashion (above); café culture is thriving in this vibrant city (below)

LOCAL CUISINE

Dressler (▷ 72): Classic dishes and and environment that harks back to a bygone age.
Henne (▷ 56): Anything you want, so long as it's roast chicken.
Luisen-Bräu (▷ 28): Brewery restaurant with its own first-class liquid accompaniment.
Marjellchen (▷ 38): Tastes of the East (of Germany).

BEST OF ABROAD

Ana e Bruno (▷ 28): Modern Italian classics.
Facil (▷ 48): Mediterranean airs and graces.
Sixties (▷ 86): Great burgers 'n' fries—what else?—US-style.
Frida Kahlo (▷ 94): Fantastic Mexican food.

Many hotels retain classic features (below); take in some blues at one of the city's jazz clubs (middle)

HOTELS OF CHARACTER

Esplanade Grand Hotel (▷ 112): The best of Berlin.

Hansablick (▷ 110): Works of art and views of the Spree.

Luisenhof (▷ 111): Housed in a restored building dating from 1822.

Hotel–Pension Savoy (▷ 111): Fine baroque columns feature here.

HOT AND COOL

A-Trane Jazz Club (▷ 37): Noteworthy modern jazz.

Chez Nous (▷ 37): Gender lines are blurred at this renowned transvestite show.

Kesselhaus (▷ 93): Dance the night away in a former brewery.

BRIGHT LIGHTS

Berliner Ensemble (▷ 71): Bertolt Brecht set the stage here.

Deutsche Oper (▷ 27): None but the finest notes and steps.

Philharmonie (▷ 47): Ultramodern home base of the Berlin Philharmonic Orchestra.

A striking modern mosaic greets visitors at the reception of the Hotel Transit Loft (above)

LOOKING FOR A BARGAIN

Hotel Transit Loft (▷ 109): Better-than-average class and facilities.

Trödelmarkt Strasse des 17. Juni (▷ 36): Have a rummage and you might just pick up that valuable antique for a song.

Wannsee-Kladow ferry (▷ 106): Take a relaxing cruise with a public transport Tageskate.

The minimalist bar and reception area of the Hotel Transit Loft in Prenzlauer Berg (left)

PAMPERED LIFESTYLES

Villa Grisebach (▷ 36): Bargain-basement art is not to be expected.
Kempinski Hotel Bristol (▷ 112): Indulge yourself at this luxury hotel.
Schloss Sanssouci (▷ 104): How Prussian royalty lived it up.

Relax and be pampered (below); designed by Langhans' Brandenburger Tor (middle)

ACTIVITIES FOR KIDS

Filmpark Babelsberg (▷ 101): Go behind the scenes at a movie studio.
Sea Life Berlin (▷ 83): Dive into the depths of the underwater world.
Zeiss-Grossplanetarium (▷ 106): See the stars in their eyes.
Zoo Berlin (▷ 34): Visit the zoo and aquarium here.

WORLD WAR II SITES

Brandenburger Tor (▷ 60): See where the Nazis held triumphal military processions.
Gedenkstätte Deutscher Widerstand (▷ 45): Visit the headquarters of the army officers who led the failed 1944 July Plot against Hitler.
Denkmal für die Ermordeten Juden Europas (▷ 69): Contemplate the monument to the six-million Jewish victims of the Nazi terror.
Kaiser-Wilhelm-Gedächtniskirche (▷ 32): Pass a few moments in quiet contemplation at this bombed-out cathedral.

REVISITING THE COLD WAR

Checkpoint Charlie (▷ 61, 70): See an adjacent surviving section of the Berlin Wall.
Glienicker Brücke (▷ 105): Discover where spies were swapped.
Rathaus Schöneberg: Stand in the spot where President Kennedy famously declared: "Ich bin ein Berliner."

Signs remain from the Cold War days at Checkpoint Charlie (above)

The Glienicker Bridge is now the principal border-crossing point into Germany (right)

Berlin by Area

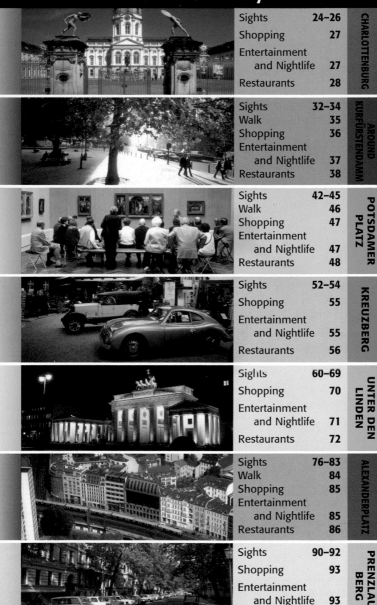

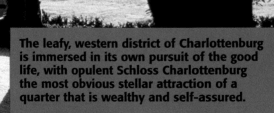

The leafy, western district of Charlottenburg is immersed in its own pursuit of the good life, with opulent Schloss Charlottenburg the most obvious stellar attraction of a quarter that is wealthy and self-assured.

Charlottenburg

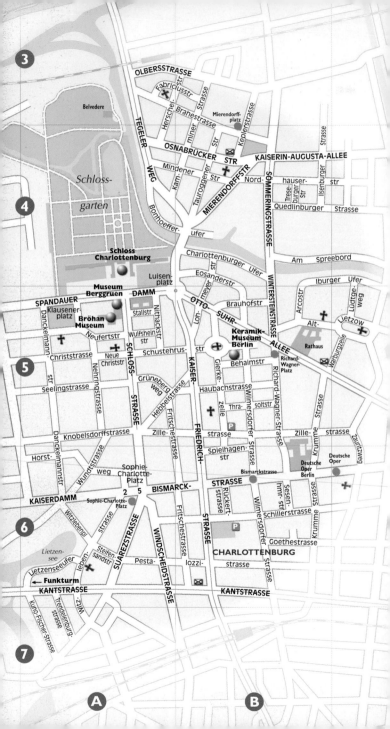

0   250 m
0   250 yds

C   **D**   **E**

Schloss Charlottenburg

This attractive former royal palace, built in the rococo style, lies in grounds only a stone's throw from the heart of Berlin. The highlights of the Schloss itself have to be the gorgeous White Hall and Golden Gallery, in the New Wing.

Royal retreat The Schloss was built over more than 100 years, and its development mirrors the aggrandizement of the Prussian dynasty of Hohenzollern, recalled in the forecourt by Andreas Schlüter's superb equestrian statue of the Great Elector; it once stood outside the Berlin Schloss. The Electress Sophie Charlotte's rural retreat—this suburb of Berlin was still deep in the countryside and considered suitable for a summer palace—designed by Johann Arnold Nering in 1695, was transformed into the palace you see today during

This restored Prussian palace (left) was built as a summer retreat for Queen Charlotte; decoration on the palace entrance gates (top right); the Galerie der Romantik on the ground floor has a collection of 19th-century artists' work, including Heinrike Dannecker *by Schick (middle) and* Landscape with Apollo *by Philip Hackert (right)*

the reigns of Frederick I and Frederick II by the architect Georg Wenzeslaus von Knobelsdorff. The Great Orangery and Theater form wings of the palace, as does the Langhans Building, at the western end of the Orangery.

Riverside grounds Do not leave Schloss Charlottenburg without seeing the delightful grounds, which slope towards the River Spree. The formal French garden is a marked contrast to the landscaped English garden, which houses the Mausoleum built for Queen Luise, and the Belvedere, now a museum devoted to Berlin porcelain. Closer to the palace, do not miss the delightfully idiosyncratic Neue Pavillon, designed by Berlin's best-known 19th-century architect, Karl Friedrich Schinkel. Today the palace gardens are a popular public park.

THE BASICS

www.spsg.de

➕ A4

✉ Spandauer Damm

☎ 030 32 09 10

🕐 Altes Schloss: Apr–Oct Tue–Sun 10–6; Nov–Mar 10–5. Neuer Flügel: Apr–Oct Wed– Mon 10–6; Nov–Mar 10–5

🍴 Restaurant

Ⓤ U-Bahn Richard-Wagner-Platz, Sophie-Charlotte-Platz

🚌 M45, 109, 309

♿ Few

💲 Expensive

More to See

BRÖHAN-MUSEUM

www.broehan-museum.de

In 1983, Professor Karl H. Bröhan presented his superb collection of Jugendstil (art nouveau), art deco and functionalism crafts to the city. The highlights of the museum are beautifully decorated rooms in the styles of the leading designers of the period. The porcelain collection is particularly fine.

➕ A5 ✉ Schlossstrasse 1a ☎ 030 32 69 06 00 🕒 Tue–Sun 10–6 🚇 U-Bahn Sophie-Charlotte-Platz, Richard-Wagner-Platz 🚌 M45, 109, 309 💰 Moderate

FUNKTURM

Berlin's broadcasting tower was built between 1924 and 1926. It reaches up 150m (492ft) above the Messe-gelände Congress Center, and has a restaurant (▷ 28) at 55m (180ft), and a viewing platform at 126m (413ft) that has fine views.

➕ Off map A6 ✉ Messedamm 22 ☎ 030 30 38 29 00 🕒 Mon 10–8, Tue–Sun 10am–11pm 🚇 S-Bahn Messe Nord/ICC 🚌 M49, X34, 104, 139, 218 💰 Moderate

KERAMIK-MUSEUM BERLIN

www.keramik-museum-berlin.de

Tucked away in a town house dating from 1712 on a side street not far from Schloss Charlottenburg, the Ceramic Museum is something of a labor of love. The permanent collection covers many periods, from antique to modern, and is supported by temporary exhibitions.

➕ B5 ✉ Schustehrusstrasse 13 ☎ 030 321 2322 🕒 Fri–Mon 1–5 🚇 U-Bahn Richard-Wagner-Platz 💰 Inexpensive

MUSEUM BERGGRUEN

www.smb.museum

A stimulating exhibition of paintings and sculptures by Picasso and his contemporaries. There are some 100 pieces by Picasso and works by Klee, Matisse, Braque, Giacometti and Cézanne. The Picassos include works that cover his artistic career, both in time and in the many styles he adopted.

➕ A5 ✉ Schlossstrasse 1 ☎ 030 266 42 42 42 🕒 Tue–Fri 10–6, Sat–Sun 11–6 🚇 U-Bahn Sophie-Charlotte-Platz 💰 Moderate

The 20th-century Funkturm (left)

The Rotunda of the Museum Berggruen (below)

Shopping

BOOKS IN BERLIN
There is a wide spectrum of English-language books to choose from here, both new and secondhand, from classical and modern fiction to history, politics, reference and travel.
➕ C6 ✉ Goethestrasse 69 ☎ 030 313 12 33 🚇 S-Bahn Savignyplatz

GIPSFORMEREI
This is the place to come for top-quality plaster reproductions of famous items from Berlin's museums, such as a bust of Queen Nefertiti.
➕ Off map, just west of A5 ✉ Sophie-Charlotten-Strasse 17–18 ☎ 030 326 76 90 🚇 S-Bahn Westend

HARRY LEHMANN
In business since 1926, this family-owned shop creates and sells good, moderately priced, non-designer perfumes from secret recipes.
➕ B6 ✉ Kantstrasse 106 ☎ 030 324 35 82 🚇 U-Bahn Wilmersdorfer Strasse

KÖNIGSBERGER MARZIPAN WALD
This long-running, family confectioners is the place to come for traditional Königsberger marzipan.
➕ A6 ✉ Pestalozzistrasse 54a ☎ 030 323 82 54 🚇 U-Bahn Sophie-Charlotte-Platz

Entertainment and Nightlife

CAFÉ THEATER SCHALOTTE
This one-time movie theater has been artfully transformed into a venue for alternative theater, cabaret and music, and has a foyer café.
➕ B5 ✉ Behaimstrasse 22 ☎ 030 341 14 85 🚇 U-Bahn Richard-Wagner-Platz

DEUTSCHE OPER BERLIN
www.deutscheoperberlin.de
The wonderful Deutsche Oper company has been staging classical and modern opera and ballet, plus symphony and chamber concerts since 1912. Performances since World War II have been held in Fritz Bornemann's contemporary glass-fronted building. Even in the cheap seats you get a great view and can appreciate the fine acoustics.
➕ B6 ✉ Bismarckstrasse 35 ☎ 030 343 84 01; tickets 030 343 84 343 🕐 Mon–Sat 11–1 and 1 hour before performance, Sun 10–2 and 1 hour before performance 🚇 U-Bahn Deutsche Oper

WILHELM HOECK
Settle down to enjoy a glass of foaming pilsner beer amid the smoky hubbub and venerable surroundings of this neighborhood *Kneipe* that's been a popular watering hole and Charlottenburg institution since 1892.
➕ B6 ✉ Wilmersdorfer Strasse 149 ☎ 030 341 81 74 🚇 U-Bahn Bismarckstrasse

DIE WÜHLMÄUSE
Generating belly laughs since the 1960s for its sardonic treatment of German political life and social mores, this renowned comedy cabaret now occupies a superb theater in the 1920s modernist Amerikahaus.
➕ Off map, west of A6 ✉ Pommernallee 2–4 ☎ 030 306 730 11 (for tickets) 🚇 U-Bahn Theodor-Heuss-Platz

---

LOCAL BARS
Nowhere do many Berliners feel so much at home as in their friendly local *Kneipe*—except, maybe, actually at home. These local bars take seriously their mission to sell decent, if rarely adventurous, local food alongside the drinks, providing a service that separates them from a *Bierstube* (pub).

Restaurants

PRICES

Prices are approximate, based on a 3-course meal for one person.
€€€ over €40
€€ €20–€40
€ under €20

ALT-LUXEMBURG (€€€)

One of the best French restaurants in the city—and then there are the German and European variations. Celebrity Chef Karl Wannemacher presides over his elegant temple of taste.

➕ A6 ✉ Windscheidstrasse 31 ☎ 030 323 87 30 🕐 Mon–Sat 5pm–midnight 🚇 U-Bahn Sophie-Charlotte-Platz

ANA E BRUNO (€€€)

Adventurous and experimental, this restaurant goes above and beyond Italian classics to create a modern cuisine style with a menu that changes monthly using seasonal ingredients.

➕ Off map, west of A5 ✉ Sophie-Charlotten-Strasse 101 ☎ 030 325 71 10 🕐 Daily 5pm–midnight 🚇 S-Bahn Westend

FUNKTURM RESTAURANT (€€)

From a point 55m (180ft) high on the Radio Tower (▷ 26), the view outside is matched by 1920s-style decor inside and breezy yet refined continental cuisine and service.

➕ Off map, west of A6 ✉ Messedamm 22 ☎ 030 30 38 29 00 🕐 Tue 6pm–11pm, Wed–Sun 11.30–11 🚇 S-Bahn Messe Nord/ICC

GOOD FRIENDS (€€)

This is the place to go in Charlottenburg for delicious Cantonese dishes and specialties.

➕ C6 ✉ Kantstrasse 30 ☎ 030 313 26 59 🕐 Daily 12pm–1am 🚇 S-Bahn Savignyplatz

ISTANBUL (€€)

Considered by many locals to be the finest Turkish eatery in town. It's not cheap but the food is authentic and the service friendly.

➕ B6 ✉ Pestalozzistrasse 84 ☎ 030 883 27 77 🕐 Daily 10am–midnight 🚇 U-Bahn Wilmersdorfer Strasse

TAXES, SERVICE AND TIPPING

Bills include a 19 percent value-added tax—officially, *Umsatzsteuer* (USt), but commonly known as *Mehrwertsteuer* (MwSt). In many restaurants there is a service charge (*Bedienung*), generally of 15 percent; this should be clear from the menu. If it's included there is no need to leave a full tip; rounding up by a few euros will suffice. When it's not included, or you want to tip for good service, leaving around 10 percent is usual.

LUISEN-BRÄU (€€)

The Luisen-Bräu brewery's in-house eatery is committed to traditional German food. Naturally excellent beer provides the perfect accompaniment.

➕ B4 ✉ Luisenplatz 1 ☎ 030 341 93 88 🕐 Sun–Thu 9am–1am, Fri–Sat 9am–2am 🚇 U-Bahn Richard-Wagner-Platz

PARAS (€€)

Try the delicious samosas with three different sauces at this simple and unobtrusive Indian restaurant.

➕ B7 ✉ Giesebrechtstrasse 19 ☎ 030 308 31 418 🕐 Daily 12–12 🚇 U-Bahn Adenauerplatz

SCHNITZELEI (€€)

Putting traditional Alpine cuisine in a modern-design setting might be counterintuitive, but it works. Dishes are served tapas-style, and there are vegetarian options.

➕ C5 ✉ Röntgenstrasse 7 ☎ 030 34 70 27 78 ☎ Mon–Fri 4pm–midnight, Sat–Sun 12–12 🚇 U-Bahn Richard-Wagner-Platz

TOKYO HAUS (€€)

Sushi and teppanyaki are both freshly prepared and served at this Japanese restaurant that doesn't allow its mastery of showmanship to get in the way of traditional craft.

➕ B8 ✉ Brandenburgischle Strasse 30 ☎ 030 88 70 79 89 ☎ Daily 12–12 🚇 U-Bahn Adenauerplatz

The great boulevard Kurfürstendamm is known locally as the "Ku'damm." There's far more to the bustling Ku'damm district than its renowned thoroughfare, however, as a stroll into its busy "hinterland" will confirm.

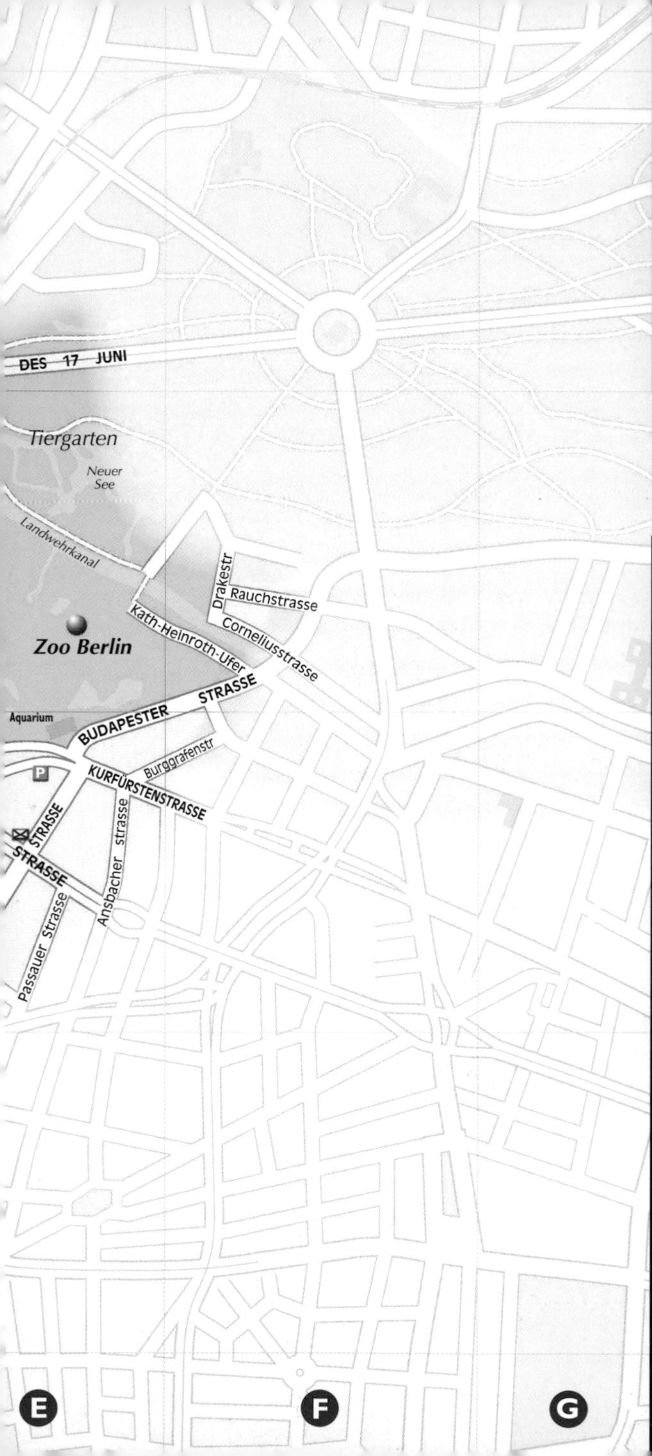

DES 17 JUNI

Tiergarten

*Neuer
See*

Landwehrkanal

Drakestr

Rauchstrasse

Kath-Heinroth-Ufer

Corneliusstrasse

Zoo Berlin

Aquarium

BUDAPESTER STRASSE

Burggrafenstr

KURFÜRSTENSTRASSE

STRASSE

STRASSE

Passauer Strasse

Ansbacher strasse

E F G

Kaiser-Wilhelm-Gedächtniskirche

The bomb-damaged original church now stands as a war memorial

THE BASICS

www.gedaechtniskirche-berlin.de

➕ E7

✉ Breitscheidplatz

☎ 030 218 50 23

🕐 Memorial Hall: Mon–Sat 10–4. New Chapel: daily 9–7

🚇 U- or S-Bahn Zoologischer Garten, U-Bahn Kurfürstendamm

🚌 X9, X10, X34, M19, M29, M46, 100, 109, 110, 145, 200, 204, 205

♿ Few 🆓 Free

HIGHLIGHTS

● Cross of nails
● Surviving mosaics
● The Stalingrad Madonna
● Bell tower
● Globe Fountain

TIP

● Even if you are not particularly religious, it can be interesting to attend one of the short services (some in English) at the church.

The blackened ruin of this church—bombed in 1943, now a reminder of the cost of war—casts its shadow over the Ku'damm. Particularly moving is the cross of nails given by the people of Coventry, in England, another war-torn city.

War memorial The Gedächtniskirche, built in 1895 in Romanesque style, was Kaiser Wilhelm II's contribution to the developing New West End. No expense was spared on the interior, and the dazzling mosaics are deliberately reminiscent of St. Mark's in Venice. After Allied bombs destroyed the church in 1943, the shell was allowed to stand. Poignant in its way, the old building now serves as a small museum focusing on the wartime destruction.

The New Chapel Berliners have denigrated the octagonal chapel and hexagonal stained-glass tower, both uncompromisingly modern (the "make-up box" and the "lipstick tube" are the two preferred nicknames). However, many visitors find peace in the blue-hue chapel, whose stained glass is from Chartres, France. The chapel was designed by Egon Eiermann in the early 1960s.

Breitscheidplatz In marked contrast, brash Breitscheidplatz proclaims the values of a materialistic culture, only partially redeemed by the vibrant street musicians and fund-raising stunts. Nowadays it is a refuge for Berlin's down-and-outs and is routinely targeted by the police. The focus is the 1983 Globe Fountain (Weltkugelbrunnen).

Kurfürstendamm

The "Ku'damm" is the place for the latest fashions as well as chic modern art

It would be unthinkable to come to Berlin without visiting the "Ku'damm," which stretches for 3.5km (2 miles) west through Charlottenburg. The city's celebrated tree-lined boulevard is usually buzzing with pavement cafés, along with restaurants and Berlin's major shops.

Shopping street Many of the Ku'damm stores were the beneficiaries of the *Wirtschaftswunder*, the economic miracle of the 1960s, which was brought about partly by American investment.

New West End The elegant streets off the Ku'damm—Fasanenstrasse, for example—were part of the New West End, which was developed as a residential area at the end of the 19th century. Some of the houses here are now art galleries; an exception is the museum devoted to the life and work of the 20th-century artist Käthe Kollwitz at Fasanenstrasse 24. Next door to the museum is the Literaturhaus, a cultural hub with a secluded garden café, the Wintergarten. The Villa Grisebach at No. 25 is an outstanding example of Jugendstil architecture. On the corner of Leibnizstrasse is another period piece, the Iduna House, whose cupola dates from 1907.

Coffee shops Johann Georg Kranzler opened the first coffee shop in Berlin in 1835, on the corner of Friedrichstrasse and Unter den Linden. Today, tourists and literati have taken the place of the Prussian aristocracy who once frequented the many cafés; join them for a superb coffee.

THE BASICS

🔲 D7

🚇 U-Bahn Kurfürstendamm; U-Bahn Uhlandstrasse

🚌 X10, M19, M29, 109, 110

🚉 Zoologischer Garten

Literaturhaus and Wintergarten Café

www.literaturhaus-berlin.de

🔲 D7

✉ Fasanenstrasse 23

☎ 030 887 28 60

🕐 Mon–Fri 10–5; café daily 9am–midnight

🍴 Excellent

♿ Few

✋ Free

Käthe-Kollwitz-Museum

www.kaethe-kollwitz.de

🔲 D7

✉ Fasanenstrasse 24

☎ 030 882 52 10

🕐 Daily 11–6

♿ Few

✋ Moderate

HIGHLIGHTS

● Literaturhaus
● Käthe-Kollwitz-Museum
● Fasanenstrasse
● Iduna House
● The KaDeWe department store
● Neoclassical newsstands

Zoo Berlin

There's no accounting for taste—elephants enjoying a Christmas tree snack at the zoo

THE BASICS

www.tierpark-berlin.de

Zoo

➕ E6

✉ Hardenbergplatz 8

☎ 030 25 40 10

🕐 Daily 9–7 (closes earlier out of season)

🚇 U- or S-Bahn Zoologischer Garten

💷 Expensive. Joint ticket with Aquarium available

Aquarium

www.aquarium-berlin.de

➕ E7

✉ Budapester Strasse 32

☎ 030 25 40 10

🕐 Daily 9–6 (closes earlier out of season)

💷 Expensive. Joint ticket with Zoo available

HIGHLIGHTS

● Bao Bao the giant panda
● Feeding polar bears and seals
● Hippopotamus House
● Baby elephant enclosure
● Komodo dragons

Berlin's zoo has developed into one of the most important in the world, with more than 20,000 animals and 1,500 species represented.

The King of Prussia The zoo dates back to 1841, when Friedrich Wilhelm IV, the King of Prussia, donated his pheasant gardens and exotic animal collection to the citizens of Berlin. After the zoo had suffered serious damage during World War II, the director, Dr. Katharina Heinroth, began the lengthy process of rebuilding it and reintroducing animals.

The Zoo At Germany's oldest and best-known zoo moats and trenches rather than bars and cages define the outdoor enclosures, creating a sense of openness and giving visitors a good view of the animals. In the Hippopotamus House glass domes cover the steamy, climate-controlled home of the Common and Pygmy hippopotamuses. A glass wall in the viewing gallery allows you to watch them swimming under water. The polar bears and seals are also free to swim around in their homes, and the seals even have their own wave machine.

The Aquarium A huge statue of an Iguanodon, which became extinct 90 million years ago, guards the entrance here. The Aquarium is occupied by a variety of fish, frogs, lizards, snakes, crocodiles and turtles from all over the world. The Komodo dragons dominate the reptile area on the second floor. Measuring 3m (10ft) in length, they are the largest lizards in the world.

A Walk around Kurfürstendamm

Kurfürstendamm, or "Ku'damm," is Berlin's most popular shopping area. This walk also takes in the zoo.

DISTANCE: 3.5km (2.2 miles) **ALLOW:** 1.5 hours

START

END

WITTENBERGPLATZ U-BAHN STATION
✚ E7 🚇 U-Bahn Wittenbergplatz

ZOOLOGISCHER GARTEN STATION
✚ D6 🚇 Zoologischer Garten

1 Head west down Tauentzienstrasse, then turn right into Nürnberger Strasse and walk down to the zoo. Enter through the Elephant Gate at Budapester Strasse 34.

8 At the corner of Uhlandstrasse you'll find the massive homeware design store Stilwerk. Continue down Kantstrasse, then turn left onto Joachimstaler Strasse to Zoologischer Garten station.

2 Stroll through the zoo to emerge at Hardenbergplatz. Turn left, keeping Zoo Station on your right. Cross over the intersection and turn right to walk up Hardenbergstrasse.

7 Pass the legendary bars and bistros around Savignyplatz to Kantstrasse and turn right.

3 Turn left onto Fasanenstrasse. The Ludwig-Ehrhardt-Haus (home of the Chamber of Commerce) on your left is one of the most interesting modern buildings in the western part of the city.

6 Retrace your steps to Ku'damm and turn left. Stroll sedately along Berlin's most famous boulevard to Knesebeckstrasse, where you turn right. Head down to Savignyplatz, setting of the movie *Cabaret*.

4 Cross over Fasanenstrasse. On your left you'll come to the Jewish center at No. 79. It was built in 1959 on the site of the synagogue, destroyed by the Nazis in 1938.

5 Continue south. The magnificent buildings south of Ku'damm are reminiscent of the imperial era, and now contain the most elegant shops in town. At No. 23 is the Literaturhaus, which has a wonderful café.

Shopping

ART & INDUSTRY

Furniture, lamps and accessories in Bauhaus and other functionalist styles; also watches.
✚ C7 ✉ Bleibtreustrasse 40 ☎ 030 883 49 46 🚇 S-Bahn Savignyplatz

BERLINER KAFFEERÖSTEREI

The mixed aroma of roasting coffee beans, tea, cocoa and pralines emanates from this old-fashioned shop off Ku'damm.
✚ D7 ✉ Uhlandstrasse 173–174 ☎ 030 88 67 79 20 🚇 U-Bahn Uhlandstrasse

BERLINER ZINNFIGUREN

A small piece of Prussian military tradition survives here, in exquisitely detailed, hand-painted pewter figurines of soldiers from ancient times up to the 19th century.
✚ D6 ✉ Knesebeckstrasse 88 ☎ 030 315 70 00 🚇 S-Bahn Savignyplatz

BIP BOUTIQUE BARBARA NEUBAUER

Wonderfully trendy fashion for women—all in black.
✚ C7 ✉ Kurfürstendamm 200 ☎ 030 881 10 55 🚇 U-Bahn Uhlandstrasse

BLEIBGRÜN

Cutting-edge designer fashions and shoes straight off the Paris catwalk are the stock-in-trade here. Innovative, yet classic designs.
✚ C7 ✉ Bleibtreustrasse 27 and 29–30 ☎ 030 882 16 89 🚇 S-Bahn Savignyplatz

CHAPEAUX HUTMODE BERLIN

For wild but rarely wooly feminine headgear, from retro to frivolous to razor-sharp contemporary.
✚ C6 ✉ Bleibtreustrasse 51 ☎ 030 312 09 13 🚇 S-Bahn Savignyplatz

DIESEL

A large shop selling the latest lines from this international brand.
✚ D7 ✉ Kurfürstendamm 17 ☎ 030 88 55 14 53 🚇 U-Bahn Kurfürstendamm

KADEWE (KAUFHAUS DES WESTENS)

The largest department store in continental Europe. The Food Hall is a must to see the fine views from the top-floor café.
✚ E7 ✉ Tauentzienstrasse 21–24 ☎ 030 212 10 🚇 U-Bahn Wittenbergplatz

KPM

Quality porcelain bearing the hallmark of Königliche Porzellan-Manufaktur.
✚ E5 ✉ Wegelystrasse 1 ☎ 030 390 090 🚇 S-Bahn Tiergarten

MARGA SCHOELLER BÜCHERSTUBE

Long-established book-store stocking English-language titles.
✚ D7 ✉ Knesebeckstrasse 33 ☎ 030 881 1112 🚇 S-Bahn Savignyplatz

ROSENTHAL

Modern Bavarian porcelain from Rosenthal plus household objects from named manufacturers.
✚ D7 ✉ Kurfürstendamm 200 ☎ 030 886 15 74 🚇 Kurfürstendamm

TRÖDELMARKT STRASSE DES 17. JUNI

One of Berlin's largest flea markets, great for retro bargains and antiques.
✚ D5–E5 ✉ Tiergarten ☎ 030 26 55 00 96 🕐 Sat–Sun 10–5 🚇 U-Bahn Ernst-Reuter-Platz

VILLA GRISEBACH

International art of the 19th and 20th centuries, displayed in the former home of turn-of-the-20th-century architect Hans Grisebach.
✚ D7 ✉ Fasanenstrasse 25 ☎ 030 885 91 50 🚇 U-Bahn Uhlandstrasse

WINTERFELDTPLATZ

One pleasant way to while away a Saturday morning is to explore the antiques shops around Motzstrasse, before homing in on one of Berlin's most vibrant and particularly entertaining street markets, in Winterfeldtplatz. You never know quite what you will find here, which is the main attraction—everything from hand-me-down jewelry to books with faded covers, from flowers to pretty children's clothes.

Entertainment and Nightlife

A-TRANE JAZZ CLUB

This lively buzzing Charlottenburg night haunt caters to lovers of modern jazz and bebop.
⊞ C6 ✉ Bleibtreustrasse 1 ☎ 030 313 25 50 🚇 S-Bahn Savignyplatz 🚌 X34, M49

BAR JEDER VERNUNFT

It's a long way psychologically from the anarchic watering holes of Mitte, Kreuzberg and Prenzlauer Berg, but this bar-cum-theater has its own play book, and serves up drinks, music and cabaret.
⊞ D8 ✉ Schaperstrasse 24 ☎ 030 883 15 82 🚇 U-Bahn Spichernstrasse

CAFÉ KEESE

Something of a Berlin institution, this rather formal dance café has phones on the tables; men and women each get their chance to choose a partner.
⊞ C6 ✉ Bismarckstrasse 108 ☎ 030 312 91 11 🚇 U-Bahn Ernst-Reuter-Platz

CASCADE CLUB

Browse 250 different cocktails at this chic new arrival on the scene, and dance to house, R&B, and 70s and 80s disco classics at the Friday and Saturday club nights.
⊞ D7 ✉ Fasanenstrasse 81 ☎ 030 31 80 09 40 🚇 U- or S-Bahn Zoologischer Garten

CHEZ NOUS

Famous for its transvestite shows, and still going strong

after more than 30 years. Reserve well in advance.
⊞ E7 ✉ Marburger Strasse 14 ☎ 030 213 18 10 🚇 U-Bahn Kurfürstendamm

MOMMSEN-ECK

This traditional wood-rich pub with a friendly atmosphere has been serving more than 100 types of beer for over a century.
⊞ C7 ✉ Mommsenstrasse 45 ☎ 030 324 25 80 🚇 S-Bahn Charlottenburg

QUASIMODO

Stifling and crowded, this is a good place to hear live jazz, blues and funk. Reduced-price tickets are available up to one day before the performance. Live music from 10pm.
⊞ D7 ✉ Kantstrasse 12a ☎ 030 3100 45 60 🚇 U- or S-Bahn Zoologischer Garten

GOODBYE TO CABARET

The 1920s was the undisputed golden age of cabaret, a fact seized on by Bob Fosse in his 1972 film musical *Cabaret*, based on Christopher Isherwood's novel *Goodbye to Berlin*. The main characteristics of the art form were biting political satire and unabashed sexual license. Since World War II, Berliners have done their best to revive the tradition but the modern clubs are often more like variety shows —the bite is missing.

DIE STACHELSCHWEINE

The satire (in German) at "The Porcupines" cabaret is famously prickly and the targets widespread, both domestic and overseas.
⊞ E7 ✉ Europa-Center, Tauentzienstrasse 9–12 ☎ 030 261 47 95 🚇 U-Bahn Kurfürstendamm

THE STORY OF BERLIN

This state-of-the-art exhibition uses 3-D sound systems, touch screens, time tunnels and adventure rooms to tell the story of Berlin since 1237.
⊞ D7 ✉ Kurfürstendamm 207–208, Ku'damm Karree ☎ 030 88 72 01 00 🕐 Daily 10–8 🚇 U-Bahn Uhlandstrasse 💲 Expensive (family card available)

THEATER DES WESTENS

A graceful theater dating from 1896 is the place to go for big-budget spectacles and translations of Broadway and West End musicals.
⊞ D7 ✉ Kantstrasse 12 ☎ 030 31 90 30 🚇 U- and S-Bahn Zoologischer Garten

TIMES BAR

Named after the Times of London, this bar is a homey place to settle down in with a newspaper.
⊞ D7 ✉ Savoy Hotel, Fasanenstrasse 9–10 ☎ 030 31 10 30 🚇 U-Bahn Uhlandstrasse

Restaurants

PRICES

Prices are approximate, based on a 3-course meal for one person.
€€€ over €40
€€ €20–€40
€ up to €20

CAFÉ AEDES-WEST (€€)
A trendy spot for those who want to see and be seen.
🕀 C7 ✉ Bleibtreustrasse 5A ☎ 030 31 50 95 35 🕓 Mon–Fri 8am–midnight, Sat–Sun 9am–midnight 🚇 S-Bahn Savignyplatz

DIENER TATTERSAAL (€€)
You are guaranteed to get a warm welcome at this homey old-style Berlin pub serving top-notch Austrian cuisine.
🕀 D7 ✉ Grolmanstrasse 47 ☎ 030 881 53 29 🕓 Daily 6pm–3am 🚇 S-Bahn Savignyplatz

HUGOS (€€€)
The haute cuisine prepared by Chef Thomas Kammeier has been awarded one Michelin star—one of only a few of Berlin's restaurants to receive the accolade. Worth it for the splendid panoramic views over Berlin from the roof.
🕀 F6 ✉ Hotel InterContinental, Budapester Strasse 2 ☎ 030 26 02 12 63 🕓 Tue–Sat 6.30pm–10.30 🚇 U- and S-Bahn Zoologischer Garten

KARTOFFELKISTE (€€)
Tuck into wholesome and hearty German cooking at this restaurant dedicated to the humble potato. Every dish contains potato in some shape or form, and that includes the pizza bases.
🕀 E7 ✉ Europa-Center, 1 Etage ☎ 030 261 42 54 🕓 Mon–Thu and Sun 11.30–10pm, Fri–Sat 11.30am–11pm 🚇 U- and S-Bahn Zoologischer Garten

KNESE (€€)
For a taste of the Berlin cuisine of yesteryear, head for this stylishly old-fashioned restaurant for some *Königsberger Klopse* (meatballs) and calf's liver with apple sauce.
🕀 D7 ✉ Knesebeckstrasse 63 ☎ 030 884 134 48 🕓 Daily noon–1am 🚇 U-Bahn Uhlandstrasse

AT THE WÜRSTCHENBUDE

Sausage stands (*Würstchenbuden*) and snack bars (*Schnellimbisse*) are popular in Germany, and usually offer *Thüringer Bratwurst* (grilled sausage), the spicier *Krakauer* and *Frankfurter Bockwurst* and *Currywurst* (fried sausage with curry ketchup). Other snacks include hamburger meatballs, served hot or cold, and called *Buletten* in Berlin.

LUTTER & WEGNER (€€–€€€)
This charming south German and Austrian restaurant includes *Tafelspitz* and *Wiener Schnitzel*. Daily specials are chalked up on a board.
🕀 C7 ✉ Schlüterstrasse 55 ☎ 030 881 34 40 🕓 Tue–Sun 6pm–11.30pm 🚇 S-Bahn Savignyplatz

MARJELLCHEN (€€)
It's hard to experience more traditional dining than at this much-loved local institution, which specializes in the hearty dishes of Germany's lost eastern lands.
🕀 B7 ✉ Mommsenstrasse 9 ☎ 030 883 26 76 🕓 Daily from 5pm 🚇 S-Bahn Savignyplatz

SOUPKULTUR (€)
The last word in snacks and tasty soups makes this place popular with locals and tourists alike.
🕀 D7 ✉ Kurfürstendamm 224 ☎ 030 88 62 92 82 🕓 Mon–Sat 12–6.30pm 🚇 U-Bahn Kurfürstendamm

WINTERGARTEN IM LITERATURHAUS (€–€€)
This is an elegant city mansion dating from 1889 and is the setting for both the Literaturhaus and its fine continental-style café-restaurant
🕀 D7 ✉ Literaturhaus, Fasanenstrasse 23 ☎ 030 882 54 14 🕓 Daily 9.30am–1am 🚇 U-Bahn Kurfürstendamm

Squeezed between the southern rim of the Tiergarten and the waters of the Landwehrkanal, the district around Potsdamer Platz boasts a number of notable museums and war memorials.

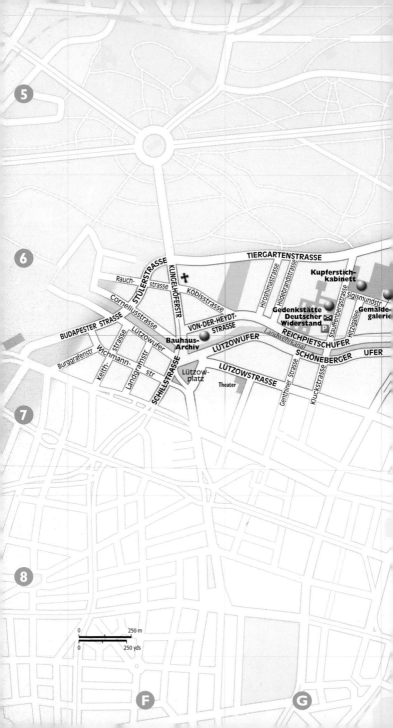

5

6

TIERGARTENSTRASSE

Rauch- STÜLERSTRASSE

KLINGELHÖFERSTR

strasse

Köbisstrasse

Cornelliusstrasse

Kupferstich-
kabinett

Hiroshimastrasse

Hildebrandstrasse

Sigismundstr

VON-DER-HEYDT-
STRASSE

Gedenkstätte
Deutscher
Widerstand

Stauffenbergstrasse

Hitzigallee

Gemälde-
galerie

BUDAPESTER STRASSE

Lützowufer

Bauhaus-
Archiv

REICHPIETSCHUFER

Burggrafenstr

Keitri-
strasse

Landgrafenstr

Wichmann-
str

LÜTZOWUFER

Landwehrkanal

SCHÖNEBERGER

UFER

SCHILLSTRASSE

Lützow-
platz

LÜTZOWSTRASSE

Genthiner Strasse

Kluckstrasse

7

Theater

8

0   250 m

0   250 yds

F

G

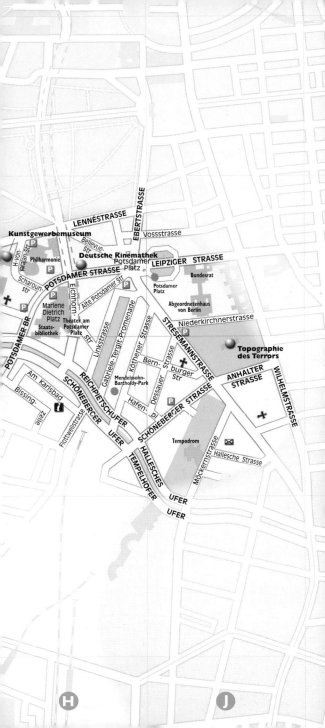

Kunstgewerbemuseum

LENNÉSTRASSE

EBERTSTRASSE

Vossstrasse

Bellevue-Str.

Deutsche Kinemathek

Philharmonie

Potsdamer Platz

LEIPZIGER STRASSE

H-von-Karajan-str

POTSDAMER STRASSE

Eichhorn-

Alte Potsdamer str

Bundesrat

Potsdamer Platz

Scharoun-str

Abgeordnetenhaus von Berlin

Marlene Dietrich Platz

Theater am Potsdamer Platz

Niederkirchnerstrasse

STRESEMANNSTRASSE

Staats-bibliothek

str

Linkstrasse

Gabriele-Tergit-Promenade

Köthener Strasse

POTSDAMER BR

Topographie des Terrors

Bern-

straße

burger

Dessauer

ANHALTER STRASSE

REICHPIETSCHUFER

Am Karlsbad

Bissing-

Flottwellstrasse

Mendelssohn-Bartholdy-Park

Hafen.

SCHÖNEBERGER STRASSE

WILHELMSTRASSE

SCHÖNEBERGER

UFER

TEMPELHOFER

Tempodrom

Möckernstrasse

Hallesche Strasse

HALLESCHES

UFER

UFER

H

J

Gemäldegalerie

HIGHLIGHTS

● *Netherlandish Proverbs,* Brueghel
● *Portrait of Enthroned Madonna and Child,* Botticelli
● *Portrait of Georg Gisze,* Holbein
● *Child with Bird,* Rubens

TIP

● The air in the gallery is kept very dry to preserve the art, but you can take a break by the water sculpture *5–7–9 Series* by Walter de Maria in the central hall.

This gallery, in the Kulturforum complex, holds some 2,700 European paintings dating from the 13th to 18th centuries. Come here to see ground-breaking works by Rembrandt, Caravaggio and Brueghel.

Various collections The Gemäldegalerie collection began by bringing together various European private collections and others from royal palaces. Following World War II, the paintings were divided between East and West Berlin. In 1965, architect Rolf Gutbrod won the competition to design a complex for the museums of European art, but building work didn't start until 1985 and Gutbrod's original drawings were reworked into what is now known as the Kulturforum. After years of planning the collection was moved to the Kulturforum and opened to the public in 1998.

Outstanding art Albrecht Dürer, Hans Holbein, Lucas Cranach the Elder and other German masters are well represented, as are the great Flemish artists Jan van Eyck, Rogier van der Weyden and Pieter Brueghel. Dutch baroque painting is also prominent, with several outstanding works by Rembrandt, among others. The Italian collection reads like a roll-call of great Renaissance artists: Fra Angelico, Piero della Francesca, Giovanni Bellini and Raphael. Outside, in the sculpture park, you can see works by Henry Moore and others. This large gallery is rather mazelike and, to add to the confusion, there are two room-numbering systems: Roman numerals for the larger inner rooms and standard numbers for the smaller rooms, called cabinets, on the outside. Pick up a map to help you get around and if you do get lost, return to the central hall to get your bearings.

THE BASICS

www.smb.museum
- H6
- Matthäikirchplatz 4–6
- 030 266 42 42 42
- Tue–Wed, Fri 10–6, Thu 10–8, Sat–Sun 11–6
- Cafés
- U- or S-Bahn Potsdamer Platz
- M29, M41, M48, M85, 200, 347
- Good
- Moderate

Bauhaus-Archiv

The clean lines of the Bauhaus-Archiv (left) are mirrored in the designs on show (right)

HIGHLIGHTS

● Walter Gropius's building
● Marcel Breuer's leather armchair
● Metal-framed furniture
● Ceramics
● Moholy-Nagy's sculpture *Light-space-modulator*
● Designs and models of Bauhaus buildings
● Paintings by Paul Klee
● Paintings by Vassily Kandinsky
● Schlemmer's theater designs
● Marianne Brandt's tea and coffee set

Brush up on the history of design by visiting one of Berlin's foremost cultural totems—a museum celebrating the Bauhaus, one of the 20th century's most influential art-and-design movements.

End of decoration In the aftermath of World War I all values, artistic ones included, came under scrutiny. In Germany the dynamic outcome was the Bauhaus school, founded in 1919 by Walter Gropius in Weimar, the capital of the recently founded Republic. Gropius and his disciples stressed function, rather than decoration, preferring modern materials such as concrete and tubular steel for their versatility and appearance.

Interdisciplinary approach Mass production guaranteed the Bauhaus an unprecedented influence on European and transatlantic architecture and design. Workshops in metalwork, print and advertising, photography, painting and ceramics were coordinated by Vassily Kandinsky, Paul Klee, Oskar Schlemmer and Laszlo Moholy-Nagy.

Legacy The revolutionary credentials of the Bauhaus drove it into conflict with the Nazis. Forced to move to Dessau and then to Berlin, the school closed in 1933 but its influence lives on in the design of furniture and appliances found in many homes today.

Exhibition The display, ranging from furniture to sketches, is housed in a small museum based on 1964 designs.

DEUTSCHE KINEMATHEK (MUSEUM FÜR FILM UND FERNSEHEN/FILM MUSEUM)

www.deutsche-kinemathek.de

A fascinating journey through the history of German film from 1895. Also includes a tribute to Marlene Dietrich.

➕ H6 ✉ Potsdamer Strasse 2 ☎ 030 30 09 030 🕐 Tue–Sun 10–6, Thu 10–8 🚇 U- or S-Bahn Potsdamer Platz ✋ Moderate

GEDENKSTÄTTE DEUTSCHER WIDERSTAND (MEMORIAL TO GERMAN RESISTANCE)

www.gdw-berlin.de

The Bendlerblock focuses on the opposition to Hitler and focuses on the 1944 conspiracy against him.

➕ G6 ✉ Stauffenbergstrasse 13–14 ☎ 030 26 99 50 00 🕐 Mon–Wed, Fri 9–6, Thu 9–8, Sat–Sun 10–6 🚇 U-Bahn Kurfürstenstrasse 🚌 M29, M48

KUNSTGEWERBEMUSEUM (TEXTILE MUSEUM)

www.smb.museum

The wide-ranging collection covers arts and crafts and interior design from the Middle Ages to the present day.

➕ H6 ✉ Matthäikirchplatz ☎ 030 266 42 42 42 🕐 Tue–Fri 10–6, Sat– Sun 11–6 🚇 U- or S-Bahn Potsdamer Platz ✋ Expensive

KUPFERSTICHKABINETT

www.smb.museum

The "engravings room" is a collection of drawings and prints by some of the great European artists.

➕ G6 ✉ Matthäikirchplatz 8 ☎ 030 266 42 42 42 🕐 Tue–Fri 10–6, Sat–Sun 11–6 🚇 U- or S-Bahn Potsdamer Platz ✋ Inexpensive

TOPOGRAPHIE DES TERRORS

www.topographie.de

This exhibition reveals the development and activities of the National Socialist SS and State Police. The new documentation department was officially opened in 2007.

➕ J7 ✉ Niederkirchnerstrasse 8 ☎ 030 25 45 09 50 (guided tours) 🕐 May–Sep daily 10–8; Apr and Oct daily 10–6 (or dusk) 🚇 U- or S-Bahn Potsdamer Platz 🚌 129, 248, 341 ✋ Free

Movie buffs will love this museum that pays homage to German film history

The Diplomatic Quarter

Tiergarten is both the old and the new diplomatic quarter of Berlin, and in recent years numerous foreign missions have settled here.

DISTANCE: 2km (1.25 miles) **ALLOW:** 1 hour

START

KLINGELHÖFERSTRASSE
✚ F6 🚌 Bus 100 Nordische Botschaften

END

POTSDAMER PLATZ
✚ J6 🚉 S-Bahn Potsdamer Platz

1 The Nordic embassy complex at the corner of Rauchstrasse and Klingelhöferstrasse accommodates the diplomatic missions of Norway, Sweden, Denmark and Finland.

2 Walk east along Tiergartenstrasse up to Hiroshimastrasse, which is marked by the enormous Japanese embassy on the corner, and turn right.

3 On your left is the Italian embassy, on your right are the regional mission of Nordrhein-Westfalen and the embassy of the United Arab Emirates.

4 Turn left at the Landwehrkanal and then left again into Hildebrandtstrasse. The big building on your right is the Ministry of Defense.

8 Back on Tiergartenstrasse, continue east, then turn right down Bellevuestrasse to Potsdamer Platz. Stop at Weinhaus Huth, one of the few buildings here to survive the war. For years it stood alone in the no-man's land in front of the wall.

7 Return to Tiergartenstrasse and carry on eastward to the Philharmonie (▷ 47). In front of the building turn right into Herbert-von-Karajan-Strasse. On your right is the Kulturforum, with its art gallery (▷ 42–43), textile museum (▷ 45) and musical instrument museum.

6 Turn right down Stauffenbergstrasse to visit the German Resistance memorial at No. 13–14.

5 Head back to Tiergartenstrasse and continue east, passing the embassies of South Africa and India, the regional mission of Baden-Württermberg and the embassy of Austria.

POTSDAMER PLATZ WALK

Shopping

KLEIDERMARKT
Secondhand clothes are sold by weight in this large warehouse near Nollendorfplatz U-Bahn station.
✛ F7 ✉ Ahornstrasse 2 ☎ 030 211 27 60 🚇 U-Bahn Nollendorfplatz

POTSDAMER PLATZ ARKADEN
The architecturally noteworthy Renzo Piano mall has 120 shops, plus cafés and restaurants.
✛ H6 ✉ Potsdamer Platz 🚇 U- or S-Bahn Potsdamer Platz

SONY STYLE STORE
Spread out over three futuristic floors you can hear music, manipulate digital images with Sony Pictures and try out the latest Playstation.
✛ H6 ✉ Potsdamer Strasse 4 Potsdamer Platz ☎ 030 25 75 11 88 🚇 U- or S-Bahn Potsdamer Platz

TRÖDELMARKT AM RATHAUS SCHÖNEBERG
A market that's popular with antiques dealers and tourists.
✛ Off map, south of E9 ✉ John-F-Kennedy Platz 🕐 Sat–Sun 9–4 🚇 U-Bahn Rathaus Schöneberg

Entertainment and Nightlife

CINESTAR IMAX
Berlin's biggest 3-D screen employs the latest technology and electronic glasses to bring you even closer to the action.
✛ H6 ✉ Potsdamer Strasse 4, Potsdamer Platz ☎ 030 26 06 64 00 🚇 U-Bahn or S-Bahn Potsdamer Platz

PHILHARMONIE
One of the world's most famous orchestras, the Berlin Philharmonic, performs in Hans Scharoun's 1960s architectural masterpiece in the Kulturforum.
The acoustics are impeccable, and tickets like gold dust so book well in advance.
✛ H6 ✉ Herbert-von-Karajan-Strasse 1 ☎ 030 254 88 999 🚇 U- or S-Bahn Potsdamer Platz

SPIELBANK BERLIN
The Spielbank Berlin, the city's only even slightly Vegas-style casino, has both gambling tables and slot machines.
✛ H6 ✉ Marlene Dietrich Platz 1, Potsdamer Platz ☎ 030 25 59 90 🕐 Daily 11am–5am 🚇 U- or S-Bahn Potsdamer Platz

VICTORIA BAR
At this chic retro cocktail bar, an impressive list of celebrity DJs and actors drink are attracted by the extensive classic cocktail menu and quality service.
✛ G7 ✉ Potsdamer Strasse 102 ☎ 030 25 75 99 77 🕐 Sun–Thu 6.30pm–3am, Fri, Sat 6.30–4 🚇 U- or S-Bahn Potsdamer Platz

WINTERGARTEN VARIETÉ
Long synonymous with late-night entertainment, the Wintergarten makes for a fun-packed evening. International variety entertainers star.
✛ G7 ✉ Potsdamer Strasse 96 ☎ 030 588 43 40 🚇 U-Bahn Kurfürstenstrasse

CINEMA
Going to the cinema is a popular pastime in Germany, but films are usually dubbed into German. If a film is showing in its original language version it should say OV (*Originalversion*) or OmU (*Original mit Untertiteln*, original with subtitles) on the poster outside the cinema. Hollywood blockbusters are usually released at the same time as they are elsewhere in Europe.

Restaurants

CAFÉ EINSTEIN STAMMHAUS (€€)

Traditional Viennese-style coffeehouse trying to re-create a prewar Berlin café atmosphere.

 F7 ⊠ Kurfürstenstrasse 58 ☎ 030 263 91 918 ⊙ Daily 8am–midnight ⊠ U-Bahn Nollendorfplatz

CAFFÈ E GELATO (€)

Eat in or take out at this fantastic café and ice-cream shop on the top floor of the Potsdamer Platz Arkaden. Choose from an extensive range of ice creams and sorbets, share a towering sundae or sample the cakes and coffee.

H6 ⊠ Potsdamer Platz Arkaden, Alte Potsdamer Strasse 7 ☎ 030 25 29 78 32 ⊙ Mon–Thu 10am–10.30pm, Fri 10am–11pm, Sat 10am–midnight, Sun 10.30am–10pm ⊠ U- or S-Bahn Potsdamer Platz

CORROBOREE (€€)

Some pretty decent tucker is on the go at this shiny, ultramodern Australian restaurant and bar—you can order a kangaroo steak from the barbecue.

H6 ⊠ Bellevuestrasse 5, Potsdam Platz ☎ 030 26 10 17 05 ⊙ Daily 11am–1am or later ⊠ U- or S-Bahn Potsdamer Platz

ELLIPSE LOUNGE (€€€)

Chef Axel Burmeister offers crossover cuisine in this warm-toned lounge-style eatery at the Hotel Esplanade. The environment is perfect for relaxing after a busy day, perhaps enjoying a light meal with fresh herbs and spices.

F7 ⊠ Lützowufer 15 ☎ 030 25 47 88 58 ⊙ Daily 12–11 ⊠ U-Bahn Nollendorfplatz

FACIL (€€€)

Mediterranean cuisine with a French twist is served at the Hotel Mandala's Michelin-starred restaurant. You'll be treated to first-class service in this tranquil glasshouse in a bamboo-filled quadrangle at the heart of the hotel.

H6 ⊠ Mandala Hotel, Potsdamer Strasse 3 ☎ 030 590 05 12 34 ⊙ Mon–Fri 12–3, 7–11 ⊠ U- or S-Bahn Potsdamer Platz

ANYONE FOR COFFEE?

Café culture continues to thrive in the capital. Sunday brunch is a weekend pastime among Berliners and indulging in afternoon *Kaffee und Kuchen* (coffee and cake) is still standard practice.

JULIUS (€€)

Under a colorful central cupola, this sophisticated restaurant has a strongly Mediterranean-influenced menu.

F7 ⊠ Hotel Berlin, Lützowplatz 17 ☎ 030 26 05 27 00 ⊙ Mon–Fri 12–3, 6–10.30, Sat 6–10.30 ⊠ U-Bahn Nollendorfplatz

KAISERSAAL (€€€)

This gourmet establishment serves superior à la carte cuisine, based on the classical German–French style. Reservations are essential.

H6 ⊠ Bellevuestrasse 1, Potsdamer Platz ☎ 030 25 75 14 54 ⊙ Daily 12–midnight ⊠ U- or S-Bahn Potsdamer Platz

VAPIANO (€€)

Ideal for a break, or for a quick but far from bland dinner, this breezy Italian chain restaurant is a cut above fast food. Tasty pasta and pizza, and some good wines.

H6 ⊠ Potsdamer Platz 5 ☎ 030 23 00 50 05 ⊙ Mon–Sat 10am–1am, Sun 10am–midnight ⊠ U- or S-Bahn Potsdamer Platz

VOX (€€€)

For a culinary feast, this restaurant serves Pacific cuisines—including sushi—and with a dab of Caribbean never far away.

H6 ⊠ Grand Hyatt Hotel, Marlene-Dietrich-Platz ☎ 030 25 53 17 72 ⊙ Daily 6.30am–midnight ⊠ U- or S-Bahn Potsdamer Platz

Kreuzberg

A multiethnic working-class community with a sizeable population of Turkish origin, Kreuzberg today has both a vibrant—and poor—character and an increasingly gentrified face in some parts.

Annen-

STRASSE

HEINE-

strasse

Michaelkitch-
platz

Dresdener

H-Heine-
Platz

Sebastianstrasse

Skallschreiber
strasse

andrinenstrasse

Walde-

Leglen-

Lelschiner-

damm

damm

ORANIENSTRASSE

Oranienstrasse

Alex-

Moritzplatz

marstr

Moritz-
platz

Naunynstrasse

Prinzessinen
strasse

Oranienplatz

ORANIENSTRASSE

Künstler-Str

Ritterstrasse

Ritterstrasse

Lobeckstrasse

STRASSE

Wassertorstrasse

Dresdener
str

Adalbert-

alexandrinenstrasse

Moritzstr

Reichenberger

Segitz

Wasser-
tor-
Platz

Kottbusser
Tor

STRASSE

GITSCHINER

STRASSE

SKALITZER

KOTTBUSSER

179

STRASSE

PRINZEN-

Prinzenstrasse

Böckerstr

Erkelenz-

Kohlfurter

strasse

Mariannen-str

Carl-

Hertz-

Ufer

Strasse

Paul-
Lincke-Ufer

Tempelherren-

str

Wilmsstrasse

Admiral-

Fraenkel-

ufer

Maybachufer

URBANSTRASSE

Geibel-
str

KREUZBERG

Plan-

ufer

Dieffenbachstrasse

BLÜCHERSTRASSE

wald-
strasse

Fontane-
Prom

RASSE

mannstrasse

| 0 | 250 m |
| 0 | 250 yds |

L   M

Bergmannstrasse

Stroll down the busy main thoroughfare to feel the pulse of this bustling part of the city

THE BASICS

+ J9–L9
⊠ Kreuzberg
🚇 U-Bahn Mehringdamm, Gneisenaustrasse, Südstern
🚌 140
🍴 Many ethnic cafés and restaurants

HIGHLIGHTS

● Gneisenaustrasse
● Viktoriapark (▷ 54)
● Marheineke Markthalle
● Passionskirche
● Volkspark Hasenheide

This street skirts the southern fringe of Kreuzberg and, along with Oranienstrasse (▷ 53), is one of the two defining streets of the district. It's worthwhile also taking in nearby Gneisenaustrasse.

Rainbow residents Bergmannstrasse shows the mixed face of multiethnic Kreuzberg. It's a part of the district where people from many cultural backgrounds live and work alongside each other. Two parks act like bookends to the street's course. In the west is the small Viktoriapark (▷ 54), inside which rises the low Kreuzberg hill, crowned by a military memorial in the shape of an Iron Cross. In the east is the Volkspark Hasenheide, a former hunting preserve. Between these two green zones stretches Bergmannstrasse. The street's character changes quite dramatically from one side to the other. In the west it is bustling and commercial, on a small scale, lined with ethnic shops, restaurants and bars. This phase ends at about Marheinekeplatz, midway along, where market stalls selling food and clothing are clustered together under the roof of the Marheineke Markthalle.

Eastern reaches A playground in the square announces the start of residential east Bergmannstrasse, its southern face adjoining the grim prospect of a series of large cemeteries. In addition, there are some impressive old churches: the Passionskirche in Marheinekeplatz, the Kirche am Südstern, and the Sankt-Johannes-Basilika just around the corner in Lillienthalstrasse.

Oranienstrasse

Turkish influences are evident everywhere along this important arterial route

Like Bergmannstrasse (▷ 52) to the south, this long street runs roughly from west to east and is a defining axis of the Kreuzberg district. But Oranienstrasse is no twin of the other; rather it is residential in its western reaches and bustling in its eastern.

Turkish character In a sense Oranienstrasse has a foot in two worlds. Where it joins Kochstrasse it is virtually an extension of the city hub, with both the Berlinische Galerie, an exhibition space for modern art, photography and architecture, and the Jüdisches Museum (▷ 54) nearby. But that changes quickly to a residential area and home to the Tiyatrom, which sounds like some high-tech modern attraction but is actually the Turkish Theater of Berlin.

Kreuzberg Appropriately enough, the farther east you go, the more pronounced Oranienstrasse's Turkish character becomes. Kreuzberg has traditionally been Berlin's alternative hub, but the trendier German elements of that character have been moving out to fast-gentrifying Prenzlauer Berg (▷ 87–94), leaving behind an area defined more by ethnic minorities, primarily Turkish.

Oranienplatz Continue farther along Oranienplatz and the Legiendamm and Leuschnerdamm lead to the Engelbeck pond. At Oranienstrasse's eastern extremity is an enclave of excellent Indian restaurants (which continues beyond the Görlitzer Bahnhof) and the famed SO 36 nightclub (▷ 55).

THE BASICS

✚ K6–M7 (and beyond)
✉ Kreuzberg
🚇 U-Bahn Kochstrasse, Moritzplatz, Görlitzer Bahnhof
🚌 M29, 140
🍴 Many ethnic cafés and restaurants

HIGHLIGHTS

● Berlinische Galerie
● Jüdisches Museum (▷ 54)
● Moritzplatz
● Engelbeck

More to See

DEUTSCHES TECHNIKMUSEUM (GERMAN TECHNOLOGY MUSEUM)
www.dtmb.de
A thoroughly entertaining and well-presented exhibition in the locomotive sheds of the old Anhalter Bahnhof. See biplanes, vintage cars, model ships, and computers; and there are plenty of hands-on experiences for children; playing on computers and other gadgets. Probably the most child-friendly museum in the city.
🚩 H8 ✉ Trebbiner Strasse 9 ☎ 030 90 25 40 🕐 Tue–Fri 9–5:30, Sat–Sun 10–6 🚇 U-Bahn Gleisdreieck or Möckernbrücke, S-Bahn Anhalter Bahnhof 💷 Moderate

JÜDISCHES MUSEUM (JEWISH MUSEUM)
www.juedisches-museum-berlin.de
This controversial building, dating from 1989 and by Polish-born American architect Daniel Libeskind, contains an exhibition on German-Jewish history from the earliest times to the present day. A Jewish museum in Berlin has an appalling burden of history to shoulder. This fact is amplified by Libeskind's abrasive architecture (attached to an existing baroque building) and by sculptural and design elements like the installation titled *Schalechet* (*Fallen Leaves*, 2001), by Menashe Kadishman, which depicts more than 10,000 faces hacked out of sheet steel. But there's more than a somber message of the Holocaust to deliver. The story of Germany's long and once rich Jewish heritage is told in an imaginative, interactive way.
🚩 K7 ✉ Lindenstrasse 9–14 ☎ 030 25 99 33 00 🕐 Tue–Sun 10–8, Mon 10–10 🚇 U-Bahn Kochstrasse or Hallesches Tor 🚌 M29, M41, 248 💷 Moderate

VIKTORIAPARK
Best known for Karl Friedrich Schinkel's *Monument to the Wars of Liberation* (1813–15), this park can also be approached from a row of terraces and gardens. There are good views of Berlin from the Kreuzberg summit.
🚩 J9 ✉ Kreuzbergstrasse 🚇 U-Bahn Platz der Luftbrücke

Classic and modern at the Deutsches Technikmuseum (above); this Gothic-style monument stands on a hilltop in Viktoriapark (right)

Shopping

BAGAGE
This shop sells bags of all shapes, sizes and hues—everything from handbags and satchels to rucksacks and travel bags.
➕ K9 ✉ Bergmannstrasse 13 ☎ 030 693 89 16
🚇 U-Bahn Gneisenaustrasse

BELLA CASA
A treasure trove of Middle Eastern and Oriental household furnishings and fittings, interesting ornaments, pottery, different perfumes, an array of herbs and spices and more.

➕ K9 ✉ Bergmannstrasse 101 ☎ 030 694 07 84
🚇 U-Bahn Gneisenaustrasse

BELLADONNA
An impressive range of natural and aromatherapy cosmetics from German companies such as Lavera, Logona, Dr Hauschka and Weleda. There are also oils from Primavera.
➕ K9 ✉ Bergmannstrasse 101 ☎ 030 694 37 31
🚇 U-Bahn Gneisenaustrasse

BERGMANN
This friendly boutique brings all the latest men's and women's fashion labels together under one roof. A great place to find his 'n' hers fashion.
➕ J9 ✉ Bergmannstrasse 2 ☎ 030 694 03 90
🚇 U-Bahn Gneisenaustrasse

TÜRKISCHER MARKT
An intriguing market in the heart of the Turkish community, offering a delicious range of choice ethnic food—including olives, cheeses and spiced chicken.
➕ M8 ✉ Maybachufer
🕐 Tue–Fri 11–6.30
🚇 U-Bahn Schönleinstrasse

Entertainment and Nightlife

GOLGATHA
This popular beer garden at the southwestern end of Viktoriapark turns into a disco at 10pm.
➕ Off map at J9
✉ Dudenstrasse 40 ☎ 030 785 24 53 🕐 Apr–Sep daily 10am–6am 🚇 U-Bahn Platz der Luftbrücke

HOPPETOSSE
Moored on the Spree, this motor ship is a restaurant by day and a club by night, with a varied diet of dancing and live music on the menu.
➕ Off map, east of M8
✉ Eichenstrasse 4 ☎ 030 69 51 89 42 🕐 Tue–Sun between 6 pm and 10pm until late 🚇 S-Bahn Treptower Park

MEHRINGHOF-THEATER
Specializes in radical or alternative cabaret. Some performances are at least partly in English.
➕ Off map at J9

LOCAL TIPPLES
A local drink is *Berliner Weisse*, beer with a dash of raspberry or woodruff syrup (*mit Grün*). More trendy is *Herva mit Mosel*, a peculiar blend of white wine with maté tea, and Berliners consume millions of glasses of the drink are annually. Hardened drinkers prefer *Korn*, frothy beer with a schnapps chaser.

✉ Gneisenaustrasse 2a ☎ 030 691 50 99
🚇 U-Bahn Mehringdamm

ROTE HARFE
The Red Harp is a lively modern café—warm, welcoming and a touch sophisticated. The weekend brunch is excellent.
➕ Off map, east of M7
✉ Oranienstrasse 13 ☎ 030 618 44 46 🕐 Daily 10am–late 🚇 U-Bahn Görlitzer Bahnhof

SO 36
Great music, from techno, Asian vibes, 1980s revival, hip-hop and house, plus some bands.
➕ M7 ✉ Oranienstrasse 190 ☎ 030 61 40 13 06 🕐 Daily between 6pm and 10pm until late 🚇 U-Bahn Kottbusser Tor

Restaurants

AMRIT (€€)

The warm surroundings, attentive staff and excellent food make this Indian restaurant a constant popular choice for both locals and visitors.

➕ Off map, east of M7 ✉ Oranienstrasse 202 ☎ 030 612 55 50 🕐 Daily 12pm–1am 🚇 U-Bahn Görlitzer Bahnhof

BERGMANN CURRY (€)

This is the place to try Berlin's unusual contribution to the world of fast food—the Currywurst—basically a sausage cut into slices, smothered in ketchup and sprinkled with curry powder. The difference here is that all the ingredients are organic.

➕ K9 ✉ Bergmannstrasse 88 🕐 Mon–Sat 12am–midnight, Sun 12–9pm 🚇 U-Bahn Gneisenaustrasse

CAFÉ AM UFER (€)

This café is a great place to be when the weather is warm. Bask in the sunshine on the terrace over a coffee or refreshing iced tea, or enjoy breakfast, lunch or a light evening meal.

➕ M8 ✉ Paul-Lincke-Ufer 42 ☎ 030 61 62 92 00 🕐 Daily 11.30am–11pm 🚇 U-Bahn Schönleinstrasse

CAFÉ ÜBERSEE (€)

Frequented by Berlin night owls, this attractive café positioned on the canal bank is busy into the early hours. It serves hearty breakfasts until 4pm daily.

➕ M8 ✉ Paul-Lincke-Ufer 44 ☎ 030 61 62 67 80 🕐 Daily 8am–2am (till 1am in winter) 🚇 U-Bahn Kottbusser Tor

CASOLARE (€)

The staff are vocal and entertaining at this bustling trattoria. Come here for the best pizza in Berlin, and at the best prices.

➕ M8 ✉ Grimmstrasse 30 ☎ 030 69 50 66 10 🕐 Daily 12–12 🚇 U-Bahn Schönleinstrasse

LITTLE ISTANBUL

Kreuzberg is a traditional working-class district near the middle of Berlin that now has the largest Turkish community outside Istanbul. In the bustling areas of Kottbusser Tor and Schlesisches Tor, dozens of restaurants offer inexpensive and interesting authentic Anatolian cuisine. However, as Kreuzberg becomes increasingly multiethnic, a growing range of national cuisines is to be found, among them Indian, Chinese, Japanese, Thai and North African.

HASIR (€–€€)

This plain but welcoming Turkish restaurant claims to have created the world's first döner kebab, in 1971. The *beyti* barbecued minced-lamb on a skewer has more of an Anatolian provenance.

➕ M7 ✉ Adalbertstrasse 10 ☎ 030 614 23 73 🕐 Daily 24 hours 🚇 U-Bahn Kottbusser Tor

HENNE (€€)

A long-time Kreuzberg institution, this old-fashioned pub-style establishment specializes in tender roast chicken from organically raised birds, washed down with a local beer.

➕ M7 ✉ Leuschnerdamm 25 ☎ 030 614 77 30 🕐 Tue–Sat from 6pm, Sun from 5pm 🚇 U-Bahn Moritzplatz

SUFISSIMO (€)

Enjoy freshly prepared couscous-based dishes at this café and Persian restaurant.

➕ M9 ✉ Fichtestrasse 1 ☎ 030 61 62 08 33 🕐 Daily 4pm–midnight 🚇 U-Bahn Südstern

SUMO (€€)

While working Japanese design into its café-style setting, Sumo places its main emphasis on the food, in particular an extensive range of sushi.

➕ K9 ✉ Bergmannstrasse 89 ☎ 030 69 00 49 63 🕐 Daily 12–12 🚇 U-Bahn Gneisenaustrasse

Unter den Linden

Encompassing the boulevard Unter den Linden at one end and the leafy Tiergarten at the other, this district is a study in contrasts and has a wealth of historic, cultural and architectural assets.

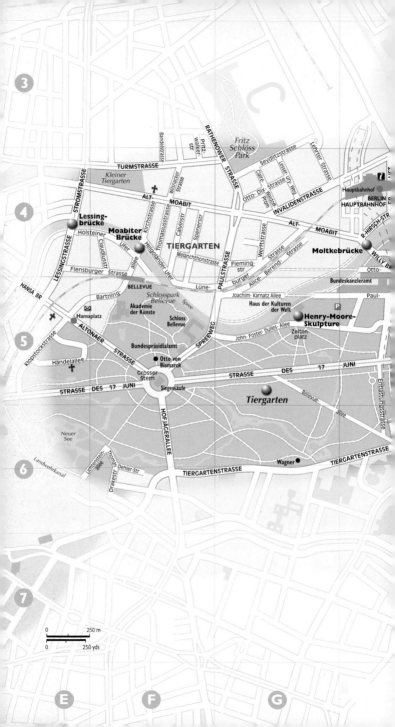

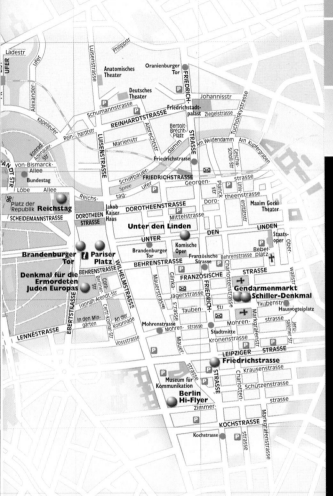

Ladestr

UFER

Alexander-

Konrad-Adenauer-Str

Kapelleufer

Pein- hardtstr

von-Bismarck-
Allee

AND STR

Löbe Allee

Bundestag

Reichs-

Platz der
Republik **Reichstag**

SCHEIDEMANNSTRASSE

**Brandenburger
Tor**

**Denkmal für die
Ermordeten
Juden Europas**

LENNÉSTRASSE

EBERTSTRASSE

Philippstr

Luisenstrasse

**Anatomisches
Theater**

**Deutsches
Theater**

Schumannstrasse

REINHARDTSTRASSE

LUISENSTRASSE

Albrechtstr

Marienstr

Schiffbauer-

Reichs- damm

Oranienburger
Tor

FRIEDRICH

Friedrichstadt-
palast

Bertolt-
Brecht-
Platz

Johannisstr

Ziegelstrasse

STRASSE

Am Weidendamm

Am Kupfergraben

Friedrichstrasse

FRIEDRICHSTRASSE

Georgen- strasse

Planck
str

Doro-
theenstrasse

Tucholskystrasse

Geschw.-Scholl-Str

Univ-erstätstr

tag

ufer

Spree

Jakob
Kaiser
Haus

DOROTHEENSTRASSE

Unter den Linden

UNTER

Brandenburger
Tor

BEHRENSTRASSE

Cora-
Berliner-Str

Hannah-Arendt Str

Gert-Kolmar-Str

In den Min-
gärten

An der
Kolonnade

Vossstrasse

DOROTHEEN
STRASSE

Mittelstrasse

DEN

Komische
Oper

BEHRENSTRASSE

WILHELMSTRASSE

Glinka

FRANZÖSISCHE

FRIEDRICH-

Jägerstrasse

Tauben-

Mohrenstrasse

Mohren- strasse

Mauerstrasse

LINDEN

Maxim Gorki
Theater

Staats-
oper

Bebel-
platz

Behrenstrasse

Französische
Strasse

Charlottenstrasse

Ober-

wallstr

STRASSE

**Gendarmenmarkt
Schiller-Denkmal**

str

Mohren-

Stadtmitte

Kronenstrasse

LEIPZIGER

Taubenstr

Markgrafenstr

strasse

Hausvogteiplatz

Jerusalemer Str

STRASSE

Friedrichstrasse

**Museum für
Kommunikation**

**Berlin
Hi-Flyer**

STRASSE

Zimmer-

Charlotten-

Krausenstrasse

Schützenstrasse

strasse

KOCHSTRASSE

Kochstrasse

strasse

Markgrafenstrasse

H   **J**   **K**

Brandenburger Tor

Gottfried Schadow's bronze sculpture tops this iconic gate

THE BASICS

- J5
- Pariser Platz
- U- and S-Bahn Brandenburger Tor
- 100, TXL
- None
- Free

HIGHLIGHTS

- *The Quadriga*
- Classical reliefs
- Adjoining classical pavilions
- View down Unter den Linden
- View down Strasse des 17. Juni
- "Room of Silence" (in pavilion)
- Pariser Platz (▷ 64)
- Tourist office and shop

The Brandenburg Gate began life as a humble tollgate, marking the city's western boundary. Today it symbolizes the reconciliation of East and West and is the perfect backdrop for commemorative events, celebrations and pop concerts.

Gate of peace? The gate is the work of Karl Gotthard Langhans and dates from 1788–91. Its neoclassical style echoes the ancient entrance to the Acropolis in Athens, on which it is fashioned. Conceived as an Arch of Peace, the Brandenburg Gate has more frequently been used to glorify martial values, as in 1933, when the Nazis' torch-light procession through the arch was intended to mark the beginning of the 1,000-year Reich.

Viktoria *The Quadriga*, a sculpture depicting the goddess Viktoria driving her chariot, was added to the gate by Johann Gottfried Schadow in 1794. In 1806, following the Prussian defeat at Jena, it was moved to Paris by Napoleon. When it was brought back in triumph less than a decade later, Karl Friedrich Schinkel added a wreath of oak leaves and the original Iron Cross to Viktoria's standard. During the heyday of cabaret in the 1920s, the goddess was often parodied by scantily clad chorus girls.

Pariser Platz During Berlin's booming 1990s, the adjoining square was transformed. Noteworthy buildings include the Adlon Kempinski Hotel, the Academy of Arts and the DG Bank.

Museum Haus am
Checkpoint Charlie (left,
middle); the former
border crossing (right)

**Named for King Friedrich I of Prussia
and laid out in the 18th century, elegant
Friedrichstrasse bisects the central city
on a north–south axis. It was itself cut in
two by the East–West cleft of the Berlin
Wall during the days of Berlin's division.**

Street of dreams Stretching from the Oranienburger Tor to the Hallesches Tor, this is a long
street, crossing the River Spree, Unter den Linden
(▷ 68) and many lesser reference points on the
way. Shoppers flock to Friedrichstrasse for retail
therapy, or alternatively partake of the area's superior dining choices. The magic word on the street
is "bargain," if you can manage to find one in its
many chic outlets. The flagship French chain store
Galeries Lafayette (▷ 70) is just one of the stellar
names. Some of the smaller streets that traverse
Friedrichstrasse, such as Französische Strasse,
have respectable shopping, dining and entertainment scenes of their own. Roughly midway
down just off its eastern face is Gendarmenmarkt
(▷ 62–63), Berlin's most handsome square and
site of the impressive Konzerthaus (▷ 71).

Cold War games Friedrichstrasse was once
one of the flashpoints of the East–West con-
frontation. The famous American Checkpoint
Charlie (▷ 18) was at the lower end of
Friedrichstrasse, at Zimmerstrasse. US and Red
Army tanks once squared off across the brief
space of that street, where tourists now snap
each other's picture, but fortunately the long-
barrel cannons remained cool.

THE BASICS

🞦 K7–J4
✉ Friedrichstrasse
🚆 U- and S-Bahn
Friedrichstrasse; U-Bahn
Oranienburger Tor,
Französische Strasse,
Stadtmitte, Kochstrasse and
Hallesches Tor
🚌 M1, M12, M29, M41,
100, 147, 200
🍴 Many restaurants
and cafés

HIGHLIGHTS

● Galeries Lafayette (▷ 70)
● Französische Strasse
● Checkpoint Charlie (▷ 18)
● Unter den Linden (▷ 68)
● Gendarmenmarkt
(▷ 62–63)

Gendarmenmarkt

This beautiful square comes as a pleasant surprise for visitors who associate Berlin with imperial bombast and Prussian marching bands. Climb the Französischer Dom tower for superb views of the Friedrichstadt district.

Konzerthaus Known originally as the Schauspielhaus (theater), the Konzerthaus was designed by Karl Friedrich Schinkel in 1821. Its predecessor was destroyed by fire during a rehearsal of Schiller's play *The Robbers*, so it is fitting that the playwright's monument stands outside. When the building was restored in the early 1980s after being severely damaged in World War II, the original stage and auditorium made way for a concert hall with a capacity of 1,850—hence the change of name. The facade,

This striking square of classic architecture draws crowds to the colonnaded Konzerthaus and the fine dome of the Französischer Dom (French Cathedral) on its far side

however, retains Schinkel's original design. Look for the sculpture of Apollo in his chariot.

Two cathedrals The twin French and German churches (Französischer Dom and Deutscher Dom) occupy opposite ends of the square. The architect Karl von Gontard was described as an ass by Frederick the Great; one of the complementary cupolas collapsed in 1781. A small museum in the Deutscher Dom charts the history of German democracy from the 19th century to the present with photographs, film and a variety of objects. A museum in the Französischer Dom tells the story of the hard-working Huguenots who settled in Berlin in the 17th century, fleeing persecution in France. The church (minus its baroque tower, a later addition) was built for them.

THE BASICS

www.franzoesischer-dom.de

✚ K5–K6

☎ Französischer Dom: 030 229 17 60. Deutscher Dom: 030 22 73 04 31

🕓 Französischer Dom: daily 10–7. Huguenot Museum: Tue–Sat 12–5, Sun 11–5. Deutscher Dom: Tue–Sun 10–6 (7 May–Sep)

🚇 U-Bahn Stadtmitte, Französische Strasse

🚌 M48, 147, 347

💷 Inexpensive

Pariser Platz

The square's organ grinders and ornate lampposts are reminders of a bygone age

THE BASICS

🕂 J5

✉ Pariser Platz

🍴 Cafés and restaurants on Unter den Linden

🚇 U- or S-Bahn Brandenburger Tor

🚌 100, 200, TXL

♿ Free

The Kennedys Museum

🕂 J5

✉ Pariser Platz 4a

☎ 030 20 65 35 70

🕐 Tue–Sun 11–7

🚇 U- or S-Bahn Brandenburger Tor

🚌 100, 200, TXL

♿ Moderate

HIGHLIGHTS

● Brandenburger Tor (▷ 60)

● Unter den Linden (▷ 68)

● Akademie der Künste

● The Kennedys Museum

● Information boards providing history and images of the square as it was in the past

Down but not out, Berlin's once beautiful 18th-century ornamental square, surrounded by palaces of the Prussian great and good, has been rebuilt along modern lines.

Risen from the ashes Once the "salon" of imperial Berlin, elegant Pariser Platz bit the dust entirely during World War II. With the onset of the Cold War and the construction of the Berlin Wall, which ran right next to it, the square was unable to recover any of its former glory. It remained a wasteland until the reunified Berlin's booming 1990s, when the square was transformed.

New look Notable modern buildings by architects, including the American Frank O. Gehry, are the Adlon Hotel, the DG Bank, the French, British and US embassies, the Akademie der Künste (Academy of the Arts) and the Dresdner Bank. There's even an airy Kennedys Museum, with an intriguing collection of historic photographs focusing on the Kennedy family's connection to Berlin. A little piece of the past remains, however, in the two rectangular gardens, each one with a fountain at its heart, that occupy the square's northern and southern quadrants.

Passing pedestrians The square was once a vibrant, lively place but now has a quieter atmosphere. There is, however, a constant stream of people shuffling to and fro between the Brandenburger Tor (▷ 60), which forms the square's western outlet, and the watering holes and cultural venues along Unter den Linden.

Reichstag

Walk to the top of Sir Norman Foster's Dome, an impressive architectural statement, to get an inside look at the seat of the German Parliament.

Parliament building The original Reichstag was built between 1884 and 1894 by Paul Wallot as the seat of the Imperial Parliament. The building was damaged by fire on 27 February 1933 and was completely devastated as a result of heavy fighting around the building during World War II. After extensive restoration, the building was handed to the Federal Administration in 1973, and the first session of the reunified Bundestag (Federal Parliament) was held here in 1990.

The Dome In June 1993, the British architect Sir Norman Foster was awarded the commission to restore the Reichstag. Foster preserved the original features and functions of the building, while adding glass walls, and a glass roof and chamber that bring light into the heart of the structure. Foster's Dome is visible for miles around and has a powerful presence on Berlin's skyline. It has also become a symbol of popular rule, and every day thousands of people climb to the top. Visitors are reflected in the central mirrored funnel as they walk up the gently sloping spiral walkway. From the top you can look down into the chamber, representing open democratic rule. There are information panels around the base of the funnel documenting the history of the Reichstag, and you can walk out of the Dome onto the roof terrace to appreciate the view over the city.

THE BASICS

www.bundestag.de
+ H5
⊠ Platz der Republik 1
☎ 030 22 73 21 52
🕐 Daily 8am–midnight
🚇 U-Bahn Bundestag
🚌 M41, 100, TXL
✋ Free

HIGHLIGHTS

● Views of the city from Sir Norman Foster's glass dome
● View a sitting of the Bundestag from the gallery
● *Black, Red and Gold* (1999) artwork of German flag in the west hall

Tiergarten

TIP

● Reaching the top of the
Siegessäule is a challenge,
but the view of the Tiergarten
district from up there should
make the climb worthwhile

**Boating, strolling, jogging, summer
concerts—this huge park in the middle
of Berlin offers all this and more,
while the diplomatic quarter south of
Tiergartenstrasse is worth exploring for
its amazing architecture.**

Hunting ground *Tiergarten* means "animal
garden," recalling a time when the park was
stocked with wild boar and deer for the pleasure
of the Prussian aristocracy. It was landscaped by
Peter Joseph Lenné in the 1830s and still bears
his imprint—remarkably, since the park was
almost totally destroyed in World War II.

Siegessäule The Siegessäule (Victory Column)
occupies a prime site on Strasse des 17.
Juni, although it originally stood in front of the

Berlin's green lung, the Tiergarten, provides an essential space for city dwellers to relax. The Siegessäule victory column (far left and detail, far right) bears scars from gunfire during World War II

Reichstag. Erected in 1873 to commemorate Prussian victories against Denmark, Austria and France, the 67m (220ft) column is decorated with captured cannon. "Gold Else," the victory goddess on the summit, beloved of Berliners, is waving her laurel wreath wryly towards Paris.

War heroes and revolutionaries The three heroes of the Wars of Unification—Count Otto von Bismarck and Generals Helmuth von Moltke and Albrecht von Roon—are fêted with statues to the north of the Siegessäule. Memorials to two prominent Communist revolutionaries, Karl Liebknecht and Rosa Luxemburg, stand beside the Landwehrkanal near Lichtensteinallee. Luxemburg's body was dumped in the canal in 1919 by members of the right-wing Freikorps who had shot both shortly after an abortive uprising.

THE BASICS

Siegessäule
✚ F5
✉ Grosser Stern, Strasse des 17. Juni
☎ 030 391 29 61
🕐 Mon–Thu 9.30–6.30, Fri–Sun 9.30–7
🚉 S-Bahn Bellevue
🚌 100, 106, 187
♿ None
💶 Inexpensive
❓ Viewing platform (no elevator)

Unter den Linden

TOP 25

The classically styled opera house (right) presides over eastern Unter den Linden (left)

HIGHLIGHTS

● Staatsoper Unter den Linden (▷ 71)
● Facade of Alte-Königliche Bibliothek
● Statue of Frederick the Great
● Humboldt University
● Neue Wache
● Zeughaus (see warriors' masks in the Schlüterhof)
● Opernpalais Unter den Linden (▷ 72)

The street "Under the Linden Trees," once the heart of imperial Berlin, has fine neoclassical and baroque buildings. The pièce de résistance is Andreas Schlüter's superb sculptures of dying warriors in the courtyard of the Zeughaus.

Forum Fridericianum Frederick the Great presides over the eastern end of Unter den Linden. His equestrian statue, by Daniel Christian Rauch, stands next to Bebelplatz, once known as the Forum Fridericianum and intended to evoke the grandeur of Imperial Rome. Dominating the square is Georg von Knobelsdorff's opera house, the Staatsoper Unter den Linden (▷ 71). Facing it is the Old Royal Library (Alte-Königliche Bibliothek), completed in 1780. Here, in 1933, Nazi propaganda chief Josef Goebbels consigned the works of ideological opponents to the flames in a public book-burning. Just south of Bebelplatz is the Roman Catholic cathedral, the Hedwigskirche, whose classical lines echo the Pantheon in Rome.

Zeughaus Frederick's civic project was never completed, but the buildings on the opposite side of Unter den Linden keep up imperial appearances. The Humboldt University was designed by Johann Boumann as a palace for Frederick the Great's brother in 1748. Next comes the Neue Wache (Guardhouse), designed by Schinkel in 1818 to complement Johann Nering's 1695 baroque palace, the Zeughaus (Arsenal). The Deutsches Historisches Museum (German History Museum) is in the Zeughaus.

More to See

BERLIN HI-FLYER
www.air-service-berlin.de
A huge, secured helium balloon rises up to a height of 150m (492ft).
➕ J6 ✉ Corner of Wilhelmstrasse and Zimmerstrasse ☎ 030 226 67 88 11
🕐 Apr–Oct daily 10–10; Nov–Mar 11–6
🚇 U-Bahn Mohrenstrasse or Kochstrasse
♿ Expensive

DENKMAL FÜR DIE ERMORDETEN JUDEN EUROPAS (MEMORIAL FOR THE MURDERED JEWS OF EUROPE)
www.stiftung-denkmal.de
This striking memorial is a field of *stelae*, through which you can stroll.
➕ J5 ✉ Between Ebertstrasse and Cora-Berliner-Strasse ☎ 030 200 76 60
🕐 Memorial permanently; Information Center Apr–Sep Tue–Sun 10–8; Oct–Mar Tue–Sun 10–7 🚇 U- or S-Bahn Brandenburger Tor
🚌 M41, 123, 200, TXL ♿ Free

HENRY-MOORE-SKULPTURE, HAUS DER KULTUREN DER WELT
Henry Moore's statue, *Large Butterfly* (1984), "flutters"

gently over a lake outside the Kongresshalle.
➕ G5 ✉ John-Foster-Dulles-Allee
🚌 100

LESSINGBRÜCKE
Scenes from playwright Gotthold Ephraim Lessing (1729–81) dramas decorate the piers of "his" bridge.
➕ E4 ✉ Lessingstrasse 🚇 U-Bahn Hansaplatz, S-Bahn Bellevue

MOABITER BRÜCKE
This bridge of 1864 is famous for the four bears that decorate it.
➕ F4 ✉ Bellevue Ufer 🚇 S-Bahn Bellevue

MOLTKEBRÜCKE
This bridge is named for a hero of the Franco-Prussian war.
➕ H4 ✉ Willi-Brandt-Strasse
🚇 S-Bahn Hauptbahnhof

SCHILLER DENKMAL
This is Reinhold Begas' superb monument to Schiller (1869).
➕ K6 ✉ Gendarmenmarkt 🚇 U-Bahn Stadtmitte, Französische Strasse

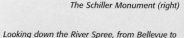

The Schiller Monument (right)

Looking down the River Spree, from Bellevue to Lessingbrücke (below)

UNTER DEN LINDEN MORE TO SEE

Shopping

BERLE'S TRENDS AND GIFTS

A great place for purchasing designer-ish personal and household gifts, for both adults and children, especially if you are not a fan of more traditional souvenirs.

➕ K6 ✉ Mohrenstrasse 50 ☎ 030 20 67 39 30 🚇 U-Bahn Stadtmitte

BERLINER ANTIK UND FLOHMARKT

Affordable antiques and bric-a-brac beneath the arches of Friedrichstrasse station.

➕ K5 ✉ Georgenstrasse ⏰ Wed–Mon 11–6 🚇 U- or S-Bahn Friedrichstrasse

BERLINER KUNST-UND-NOSTALGIE-MARKT

Art and nostalgia—for the most part paintings, drawings and antiques.

➕ K5 ✉ Am Kupfergraben ⏰ Daily 11–5 🚇 U- or S-Bahn Friedrichstrasse

BÜRGELHAUS

You will find blue-and-cream pottery from the German region of Thüringia here, at very reasonable prices.

➕ J5 ✉ Friedrichstrasse 154 ☎ 030 20 45 26 95 🚇 U- or S-Bahn Friedrichstrasse

DOM

Add a touch of sparkle to your home with kitsch accessories and lamps, or treat a friend to one of the innovative gifts from this shop.

➕ K5 ✉ Friedrichstrasse 76 ☎ 030 20 94 73 95 🚇 U-Bahn Französische Strasse

DUSSMANN: DAS KULTURKAUFHAUS

This huge book and record store is ideal for last-minute present buying. Where CDs are concerned, if they don't have it here, you won't find it anywhere. Stays open until 10pm.

➕ K5 ✉ Friedrichstrasse 90 ☎ 030 20 25 11 11 🚇 U- or S-Bahn Friedrichstrasse

FASSBENDER & RAUSCH

A luxury chocolate shop and confectioner founded in the 19th century, which still sells all manner of delicious goodies for chocaholics.

➕ K6 ✉ Charlottenstrasse 60 ☎ 030 20 45 84 43 🚇 U-Bahn Stadtmitte

---

FRIEDRICHSTRASSE

Rebuilt almost from scratch, Friedrichstrasse has become a magnet for discerning shoppers, especially aficionados of the latest designer fashions. Galeries Lafayette (▷ this page), also here, is the first branch of the famous department store outside France. Apart from Jean Nouvel's highly innovative open-plan design, the main talking point is the mouthwatering Food Hall, selling everything from pâtés to oysters.

FRIEDRICHSTADT-PASSAGEN Q205

Some 50 de luxe shops and boutiques occupy this elegant shopping mall, along with several chic restaurants and cafés.

➕ K6 ✉ Friedrichstrasse 67 ☎ 030 20 94 51 01 🚇 U-Bahn Stadtmitte

GALERIES LAFAYETTE

A branch of the iconic Parisian department store (▷ panel), and an architectural treat, too, with its impressive curved glass wall, curved roof and two glass cones inside.

➕ K5 ✉ Friedrichstrasse 76–78 ☎ 030 20 94 80 ⏰ Daily 10–8 🚇 U-Bahn Französische Strasse

HAUS AM CHECK-POINT CHARLIE

The only place in Berlin where you can still find an authentic piece of the Wall to buy; also GDR and Soviet Union medals, military insignia and much more.

➕ K6 ✉ Friedrichstrasse 43–45 ☎ 030 253 72 50 🚇 U-Bahn Kochstrasse

MEISSENER PORZELLAN

For lovers of fine china, Meissener Porzellan sells figurines and other decorative items made from the famous—and expensive—handmade Meissen porcelain.

➕ J5 ✉ Unter den Linden 39b ☎ 030 22 67 90 28 🚇 U-or S-Bahn Brandenburger Tor

Entertainment and Nightlife

ADMIRALSPALAST

During the Roaring Twenties this was the most famous theater in Berlin. Now beautifully restored, it is again a wonderful stage for concerts and musicals.

➕ J4 ✉ Friedrichstrasse 101 ☎ 030 47 99 74 99 🚇 U-or S-Bahn Friedrichstrasse

BERLINER ENSEMBLE

Playwright Bertolt Brecht founded this famous theater company in 1948. His plays are still in the repertoire.

➕ J4 ✉ Bertolt-Brecht-Platz 1 ☎ 030 28 40 80 🚇 U-or S-Bahn Friedrichstrasse

DEUTSCHES THEATER

The name of director Max Reinhardt was virtually synonymous with this theater from the turn of the 20th century until the Nazis came to power. Film star Marlene Dietrich performed here.

➕ J4 ✉ Schumannstrasse 13 ☎ 030 28 44 12 21 🚇 U-Bahn Oranienburger Tor

DISTEL

The Thistle club is known for its acerbic political satire.

➕ J4 ✉ Friedrichstrasse 101 ☎ 030 204 47 04 🚇 U- or S-Bahn Friedrichstrasse

FRIEDRICHSTADT-PALAST

This most famous nightspot in eastern Berlin has a long tradition. In the main revue, entertainment includes variety acts, a floor show and loud music; the small revue is more intimate.

➕ J4 ✉ Friedrichstrasse 107 ☎ 030 23 26 23 27 🚇 U-Bahn Oranienburger Tor

HAUS DER KULTUREN DER WELT

This modern multicultural foundation in the Tiergarten regularly hosts rock concerts and showcases African and Latin-American music.

➕ G5 ✉ John-Foster-Dulles-Allee 10 ☎ 030 39 78 70 🚇 U-or S-Bahn Brandenburger Tor

KOMISCHE OPER BERLIN

Catch modern and inventive productions of opera, dance and musical theater here.

➕ J5 ✉ Behrenstrasse 55–57 ☎ 030 47 99 74 00 🚇 U-Bahn Französische Strasse

STAATSOPER

The handsome neoclassical building dominating Bebelplatz is Berlin's oldest opera house, the Staatsoper Unter den Linden (see this page), built in the reign of Frederick the Great. It is currently engaged in a struggle with the Deutsche Oper (▷ 27), for government subsidies. Musicians who have graced this stage include the composers Mendelssohn, Meyerbeer, Liszt and Richard Strauss, and conductor Wilhelm Furtwängler.

KONZERTHAUS

The truly magnificent concert hall now housing the Berlin Symphony Orchestra was designed by architect Karl Friedrich Schinkel in 1818.

➕ K5 ✉ Gendarmenmarkt 2 ☎ 030 203 09 23 33 🚇 U-Bahn Französische Strasse

MAXIM GORKI THEATER

This theater stages plays by contemporary dramatists and works by classical German playwrights. The Gorki Studio has an experimental repertoire.

➕ K5 ✉ Am Festungsgraben 2 ☎ 030 20 22 11 15 🚇 U- or S-Bahn Friedrichstrasse

NEWTON BAR

Designer good looks extend from the racy Helmut Newton posters to the black leather armchairs—and to the cocktail-sipping clientele. Cigar fanciers can enjoy a Cuban smoke in the separate cigar lounge.

➕ K6 ✉ Charlottenstrasse 57 ☎ 030 20 29 54 21 🚇 U-Bahn Französische Strasse

STAATSOPER UNTER DEN LINDEN

The best of both homegrown and international opera and ballet are performed in a beautiful baroque concert hall.

➕ K5 ✉ Unter den Linden 7 ☎ 030 20 35 40 🚇 U-Bahn Hausvogteiplatz

Restaurants

PRICES

Prices are approximate, based on a 3-course meal for one person.

€€€ over €40
€€   €20–€40
€   up to €20

UNTER DEN LINDEN RESTAURANTS

BOCCA DI BACCO (€€€)

This is the place to go for gourmet Italian food. The food is posh, the address exclusive and the staff are friendly and welcoming.
➕ K5 ✉ Friedrichstrasse 167–168 ☎ 030 20 67 28 28 🕐 Mon–Sat 12–12, Sun 6pm–midnight 🚇 U-Bahn Französische Strasse

BORCHARDT (€€€)

With historical roots going back to 1853, this fine French restaurant is one of the most venerable dining establishments in town, though its interior design is more 1920s than 19th-century Berlin.
➕ K5 ✉ Französische Strasse 47 ☎ 030 81 88 62 62 🕐 Daily 12–12 🚇 U-Bahn Französische Strasse

CAFÉ EINSTEIN (€€)

Berlin's café tradition has been revived in an art nouveau-style interior, supported by fine coffees and teas, homemade Apfelstrudel with vanilla sauce, and a gallery for art and photographic exhibits.
➕ J5 ✉ Unter den Linden 42 ☎ 030 204 36 32 🕐 Daily 7am–10pm 🚇 U-or S-Bahn Brandenburger Tor

DRESSLER (€€)

Aims to re-create the classic dining style of 1920s and 1930s Berlin in a bustling ambience where waiters in aprons serve everything from coffee to venison.
➕ J5 ✉ Unter den Linden 39 ☎ 030 204 44 22 🕐 Daily 8am–1am 🚇 U- or S-Bahn Brandenburger Tor

LORENZ ADLON (€€€)

First-class French food, superb wines and superior service can be found in master chef Thomas Neeser's Michelin-star restaurant of the Hotel Adlon Kempinski.
➕ K5 ✉ Unter den Linden 77 ☎ 030 22 61 19 60 🕐 Tue–Sat 7pm–10.30pm 🚇 U- or S-Bahn Brandenburger Tor

LUTTER & WEGNER (€€€)

This historic 19th-century restaurant has Austrian as well as German cuisine; also a wine bar.
➕ K6 ✉ Charlottenstrasse 56 ☎ 030 20 29 54 0 🕐 Daily

GERMAN WINES

Germany is divided into 13 distinct wine-growing regions, mainly along the Rhine and Moselle river valleys. Nearly all the wine is white, relying heavily on the Müller-Thurgau and Riesling grapes. Red wines are not generally held in high esteem and not usually consumed locally.

11am–midnight 🚇 U-Bahn Französische Strasse

MARGAUX (€€€)

Fine dining at its best. Expect avant-garde creations and classic à la carte dishes at this one-Michelin star restaurant.
➕ J5 ✉ Unter den Linden 78 ☎ 030 22 65 26 11 🕐 Mon–Sat 7pm–10.30pm 🚇 U- or S-Bahn Brandenburger Tor

OPERNPALAIS UNTER DEN LINDEN (€)

Redolent of old Berlin, this palatial café with an expensive restaurant upstairs is next to the Staatsoper.
➕ K5 ✉ Unter den Linden 5 ☎ 030 20 26 83 🕐 Daily 8am–midnight 🚇 U-Bahn Französische Strasse

VAU (€€€)

Come to this superior restaurant for a menu of updated German–Austrian cuisine.
➕ K5 ✉ Jägerstrasse 54–55 ☎ 030 202 97 30 🕐 Mon–Sat 12–2.30, 7–10.30 🚇 U-Bahn Hausvogteiplatz

DIE ZWÖLF APOSTEL (€€)

Red velvet curtains, candlelight, painted ceilings and an open kitchen with fresh ingredients create a theatrical experience.
➕ K5 ✉ Georgenstrasse 2 ☎ 030 201 02 22 🕐 Mon–Thu 11am–midnight, Fri–Sat 11am–1am 🚇 U- or S-Bahn Friedrichstrasse

The UNESCO World Heritage Site of Museumsinsel is not far from Alexanderplatz. But this core of the former East Berlin, beside the River Spree, has far more to offer than just museum-hopping.

3

4

5

6

7

Linien- strasse

Grosse Hamburger

Auguststrasse

Oranienburger

Neue
Synagoge

Krausnickstr

STRASSE KL

Tuch-

Ziegelstrasse

Monbijoupark

Bode-
museum

Pergamon-
museum

Alte
National-
galerie

Am Kupfergraben

Museumsinsel

Bodestr

Altes
Museum

Am
Zeughaus

Neue Wache

Schlossbrücke

Friedrichs-
werdersche
Kirche

WERDERS-

P

LEIPZIGER

Krausenstrasse

Schützenstrasse

Zimmerstrasse

Axel-

Junkerstr

Feilner-

0   250 m

0   250 yds

H   **J**   **K**

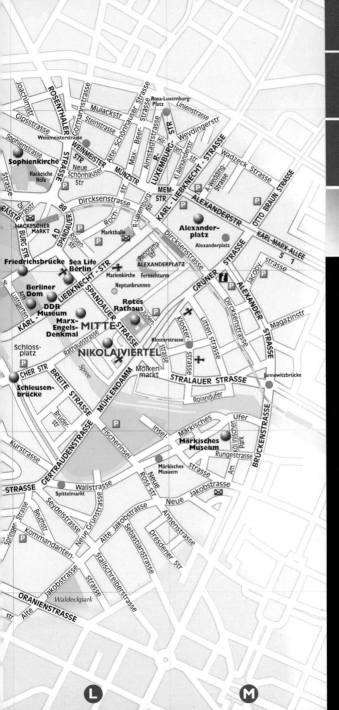

Alexanderplatz

The TV tower (left); the World Time Clock (middle) and trams (right) feature in the square

THE BASICS

www.tv-turm.de

🚇 M4

☎ Marienkirche: 030 242 44 67

🕐 Fernsehturm: Mar–Oct daily 9am–midnight; Nov–Feb 10am–midnight. Marienkirche: Apr–Oct daily 10–9; Nov–Mar daily 10–6

🍴 Cafés

🚉 U- or S-Bahn Alexanderplatz

🚌 M48, 100, 200, TXL

♿ Fernsehturm: moderate

HIGHLIGHTS

● Fernsehturm
● Rotes Rathaus
● World Time Clock
● Neptune Fountain
● Forum Hotel
● Kaufhof department store
● Marienkirche
● *Totentanz (Dance of Death)* wall painting

Once a victim of East German town planning, the "Alex," as Berliners affectionately call this historic old market place, has won back some of its charm with new and reconstructed buildings.

Historic square Alexanderplatz is named after Russian Tsar Alexander I, who once reviewed troops here. The square was colonized by Berlin's burgeoning working class in the middle of the 19th century. Crime flourished, so it is no accident that the police headquarters was nearby.

TV tower The Fernsehturm rises like an unlovely flower from the middle of the square. Its single virtue is its great height, which at 362m (1,188ft) exceeds even that of Paris's Eiffel Tower. Take the turbolift up on a fine day for panoramic city views from the viewing platform and the rotating Telecafé restaurant.

Other attractions In the square's southwestern quadrant, the spectacular Neptunbrunnen (Neptune Fountain), which was a gift to Kaiser Wilhelm II in 1891, stood originally in Schlossplatz. Its focal point is a massive bronze sculpture of the Roman god of the sea. Around the fountain's rim sit female statues representing the rivers Rhine, Oder, Elbe and Weichsel (Vistula). The Marienkirche has a 15th-century nave and a lantern tower added by Karl Gotthard Langhans in 1790. An epidemic of the plague in 1484 is commemorated in a large medieval wall painting *Totentanz (Dance of Death)*.

Berliner Dom

The ornate decoration (left), and the imposing exterior, of the Berliner Dom (right)

For evidence of imperial pretensions, look to Berlin's Protestant cathedral. The cathedral's vast vault contains the sarcophagi of more than 90 members of the Hohenzollern dynasty.

Cathedral Architect Julius Raschdorff built the Berliner Dom over the site of a smaller imperial chapel. The existing cathedral was completed in 1905 and opened in the presence of Kaiser Wilhelm II. Inside, the most impressive feature is the dome that is 74m (243ft) high, supported by pillars of Silesian sandstone and decorated with mosaics of the Beatitudes by Anton von Werner. In High Renaissance style, the dome is reached by climbing 270 steps. The cathedral was badly damaged during World War II. Restoration started in 1974 and is now well advanced. Work on the stained-glass windows has been completed.

Destroyed by Allied bombs The name of the square, Lustgarten, derives from the former pleasure garden, which stood just outside the cathedral on Museumsinsel. The site, where Prussia's first potatoes were planted in 1649, is now covered by grass and paving. Opposite, until the Allied bombings in World War II, stood the enormous Berliner Stadtschloss, dating from the early 18th century and designed by Andreas Schlüter and Johann Eosander von Goethe. The later Communist-era Palast der Republik (Palace of the Republic; 1977) has likewise been demolished. A temporary art gallery, the Temporäre Kunsthalle, now occupies the site pending reconstruction of the Berliner Stadtschloss.

THE BASICS

www.berlinerdom.de

🚇 L5

✉ Am Lustgarten

☎ 030 20 26 91 19

🕐 Apr–Sep Mon–Sat 9–8, Sun 12–8; Oct–Mar Mon–Sat 9–7, Sun 12–7

🍴 None

Ⓤ U- and S-Bahn Alexanderplatz, S-Bahn Hackescher Markt

🚌 M48, 100, 200

♿ Few

✋ Moderate

HIGHLIGHTS

- Lustgarten
- High Renaissance–style facade
- Baptism chapel
- Imperial staircase
- Sarcophagi
- Dome 74m (234ft) high
- Figures above altar
- Viewing gallery

Museumsinsel

Berlin's famed collection of antiquities is one of the city's major treasures. To see it, head for Museums Island, accessible over the Monbijoubrücke, on the Spree. The Pergamonmusuem (▷ 81) is one of five superb institutions here.

Altes Museum Built in 1830, this was the first museum on the island. Karl Schinkel's magnificent classical temple shares with the Pergamonmuseum (▷ 81) fabulous collections of sculptures from all corners of the ancient world. The impression made by the facade is overwhelming in itself, and hidden at the core of the building is a rotunda inspired by Rome's Pantheon and lined with statues of the gods.

Neues Museum Since 2009 Berlin's famed Ägyptisches Museum (Egyptian Museum) has been housed once again in this museum,

Ancient history in a modern city—the Altes Museum (left, top middle, bottom right and far right bottom) has a fascinating collection of antiquities from around the world; a highlight of the Egyptian Museum is the bust of Queen Nefertiti (top right); Berlin's Old National Gallery on Museumsinsel (bottom middle)

designed in 1843 by August Stüler. This rich collection of 2,000 ancient masterpieces spans three millennia. The highlight here is the bust of Queen Nefertiti, wife of Pharaoh Akhenaton. Dating from about 1340BC, the bust, made of limestone and plaster, was discovered in 1912 along with other royal portraits. Another highlight is the Temple Gate of Kalabsha, built by the Roman Emperor Augustus in 20BC.

Bode-Museum Named after Wilhelm von Bode (1845–1929), who for 20 years was curator of Museums Island, this 1904 building exhibits exquisite medieval sculptures, and early Christian and Byzantine art.

Alte Nationalgalerie This gallery displays mainly paintings of the 19th century, and includes works by Impressionists such as Manet, Monet, Renoir and Degas.

THE BASICS

www.smb.museum
+ K4, K5, L5
✉ Museumsinsel
☎ 030 266 42 42 42
🕐 Tue–Wed, Fri–Sun 10–6, Thu 10–10
🚉 S-Bahn Hackescher Markt, U- and S-Bahn Friedrichstrasse
🚌 100, 200, TXL
♿ Few
✋ Moderate

Nikolaiviertel

TOP 25

Bronze statues (left) and period houses (right) complement this medieval-style area

THE BASICS

www.stadtmuseum.de

L5

Poststrasse

Nikolaikirche and Knoblauchhaus: 030 24 00 21 62

Nikolaikirche and Knoblauchhaus: daily 10–6; Ephraim-Palais: Tue, Thu–Sun 10–6, Wed 12–8

U- and S-Bahn Alexanderplatz

100, 200, TXL

Few

All: moderate

HIGHLIGHTS

Nikolaikirche

- Exhibition of Berlin history
- Gothic nave
- *The Good Samaritan*, Michael Ribestein
- Hunger Cloth (in vestry)
- Wooden *Crucifixion* of 1485

Enjoy a wander through the Nikolai Quarter, a diverting pastiche of baroque and neoclassical architecture, with rows of gabled houses, cobbled streets and quaint shops.

Nikolaikirche The dominating landmark is the twin-spired church that gives the Nikolaiviertel its name. The Nikolaikirche is the oldest church in Berlin, dating originally from 1200 although the present building was not completed until 1470. Seriously damaged in World War II, the beautifully proportioned Gothic nave has been sensitively restored. The church is of great historic importance, because it was here, in 1307, that the two communities of Berlin and Cölln were formally united. The church, now used for services only occasionally, houses a museum of Berlin history.

Around the Quarter Two other notable buildings recall the lavish lifestyle of Imperial Berlin. The pink stuccoed Knoblauchhaus was designed in 1759 by Friedrich Wilhelm Dietrichs for one of Berlin's most distinguished families. The extravagant Ephraim-Palais, with golden balconies and stone cherubs, belonged to Frederick the Great's banker, Nathan Ephraim. The interior is decorated with art of the 17th to the 19th centuries.

Most picturesque Among the streets, the title probably goes to Eiergasse and Am Nussbaum, named for its cheery reconstruction of a famous 16th-century Berlin inn, Zum Nussbaum (▷ 86) ("At the Nut Tree")—a good refreshment stop.

If you have time to visit only one museum in Berlin, choose the Pergamon. Virtually every corner of the ancient world is represented, from the Roman Empire to the Islamic world.

Controversy Like the other museums on Museums Island (Museumsinsel ▷ 78–79), the Pergamon was built to house the vast haul of antiquities amassed by German archaeologists in the 19th century. Controversy rages over the proper home for such relics; some people argue that they were wrongfully plundered. Restoration of the museum began in 2008.

Pergamon Altar The museum's most stunning exhibit is the famous Pergamon Altar from Asia Minor, a stupendous monument so huge that it needs a hall more than 15m (50ft) high to accommodate it. From Bergama on the west coast of Turkey, it was excavated by Carl Humann in 1878–86. Dating from about 164BC, it was part of a complex of royal palaces, temples, a library and a theater. Hardly less impressive is the reconstructed market gateway of Miletus, built by the Romans in this town in western Turkey in AD120 during the reign of Emperor Hadrian.

Antiquities The museum also has a splendid collection of Greek and Roman statues (some of them retaining traces of their original vibrant tones), Islamic art, figurines and clay tablets. Many more objects come from Sumeria and other parts of the Middle East.

THE BASICS

www.smb.museum
K4
Am Kupfergraben, Museumsinsel
030 266 42 42 42
Mon–Sun 10–6, Thu 10–8
Café
S-Bahn Hackescher Markt; U- and S-Bahn Friedrichstrasse
100, 200, 1XL
Few
Moderate

HIGHLIGHTS

- 120m (394ft) frieze on Pergamon Altar
- Market gate from Miletus
- Ishtar Gate
- Facade of Mshatta Palace
- Nebuchadnezzar's throne room
- Figurines from Jericho
- Panel room from Aleppo
- Bust of the Emperor Caracalla
- Statue of Aphrodite from Myrina

ALEXANDERPLATZ TOP 25

More to See

DDR MUSEUM

www.ddr-museum.de

Step into a vanished world at this museum, which portrays everyday life in the Communist German Democratic Republic (East Germany). Sit in a genuine Trabbi (Trabant car), admire the dated style and much more.

➕ L5 ✉ Karl-Liebknecht-Strasse 1 ☎ 030 84 71 23 731 🕐 Sun–Fri 10–8, Sat 10–10 🚇 S-Bahn Hackescher Markt 🖐 Moderate

FRIEDRICHSBRÜCKE

This elegant bridge, built in 1892, gives a fine view of the Berliner Dom.

➕ L4–L5 ✉ Bodestrasse 🚇 S-Bahn Hackescher Markt

FRIEDRICHSWERDERSCHE KIRCHE

www.smb.museum

Berlin's celebrated architect Karl Friedrich Schinkel designed this church in neo-Gothic style in 1824. View it from the outside only.

➕ K5 ✉ Werderscher Markt ☎ 030 266 42 42 42 🚇 U-Bahn Hausvogteiplatz 🖐 Free

MÄRKISCHES MUSEUM

www.stadtmuseum.de

To visit here is to stroll back down Berlin's memory lane, from the foundation of the city in the 13th century, through its rise to Prussian and then German capital, the Nazi period, Cold War division, and reunification.

➕ M6 ✉ Am Köllnischen Park 5 ☎ 030 30 86 62 15 🕐 Tue–Sun 10–6, Wed 12–8pm 🚇 U-Bahn Märkisches Museum 🖐 Moderate

MARX-ENGELS-DENKMAL

The two founders of Communism stand shoulder to shoulder as bronze sculptures in a garden near Alexanderplatz.

➕ L5 ✉ Rathausstrasse 🚇 U-Bahn Alexanderplatz

MONBIJOUPARK

This leafy park, by the River Spree near Museums Island, has a playground and a splash pool for toddlers.

➕ K4 ✉ Oranienburger Strasse 🚇 S-Bahn Hackescher Markt

Marx and Engels Monument, Rathausstrasse

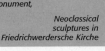

Neoclassical sculptures in Friedrichwerdersche Kirche

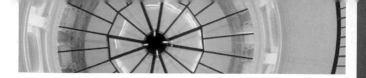

NEUE SYNAGOGE (NEW SYNAGOGUE)

www.cjudaicum.de

The stunning dome of this 1866 building is a Berlin landmark. Designed by Eduard Knoblauch and August Stüler, it was destroyed during World War II. Rebuilding finished in 1995.

✚ K4 ✉ Oranienburger Strasse 28–30 ☎ 030 88 02 83 00 🕓 Mar–Oct Sun–Mon 10–8, Tue–Thu 10–6, Fri 10–5 (Mar, Oct Fri until 2); Nov–Feb Sun–Thu 10–6, Fri 10–2 🚇 S-Bahn Oranienburger Strasse

ROTES RATHAUS

Designed by Heinrich Friedrich Waesemann, the Berliner Rathaus (Town Hall) is known as the Rotes (Red) Rathaus for its red exterior.

✚ L5 ✉ Rathausstrasse 15 ☎ 030 902 60 🕓 Mon–Fri 9–6 🚇 U- and S-Bahn Alexanderplatz 🎟 Free

SCHLEUSENBRÜCKE

This simple iron bridge is decorated with historic scenes of Berlin.

✚ K5 ✉ Werderstrasse 🚇 U-Bahn Hausvogteiplatz

SCHLOSSBRÜCKE

Karl Friedrich Schinkel designed a new bridge to replace the decrepit Hundebrücke in 1819. Named after a royal palace that no longer exists, it is decorated with statues of Greek gods.

✚ K5 ✉ Unter den Linden 🚇 U-Bahn Hausvogteiplatz

SEA LIFE BERLIN

www.visitsealife.com

Take a ride through the middle of this cylindrical domed aquarium in a glass elevator and travel into an amazing underwater world full of tropical fish.

✚ L5 ✉ Spandauer Strasse 3 ☎ 030 99 28 00 🕓 Daily 10–7 🚇 S-Bahn Hackescher Markt 🎟 Expensive

SOPHIENKIRCHE

www.sophien.de

Berlin's sole surviving baroque church, completed in 1734, was designed by J. F. Grael.

✚ L4 ✉ Grosse Hamburger Strasse 29 ☎ 030 308 79 20 🕓 May–Oct Wed 3–6, Sat 3–5 🚇 S-Bahn Hackescher Markt

Schlossbrücke is located between Schlossplatz and the avenue Unter den Linden (above); bridge marble sculpture detail (right)

Berlin Mitte

This walk takes heads through a part of town that was once at the heart of the former East Berlin.

DISTANCE: 5km (3.1 miles) **ALLOW:** 2 hours

START

STAATSOPER UNTER DEN LINDEN
🚏 K5 🚌 100, 200

END

BRANDENBURGER TOR (▷ 60)
🚏 J5 🚇 U- or S-Bahn Brandenburger Tor

1 From the opera house (▷ 71), head east along Unter den Linden.

2 Walk through the Lustgarten in front of the Berliner Dom down to Bodestrasse. Cross the Spree and turn left into Burgstrasse, past Monbijoupark (▷ 82).

3 Turn right into Oranienburger Strasse, then left into Grosse Hamburger Strasse. On the left are the remains of the Alte Jüdische Friedhof. Past 18th-century Sophienkirche (▷ 83), turn right into Sophienstrasse. Between Sophienstrasse and Oranienburgerstrasse are the historic courtyards known as the Hackesche Höfe (▷ 85); nowadays they accommodate trendy restaurants, art galleries and theaters.

4 At the end of Sophienstrasse turn right into Rosenthaler Strasse, which becomes Spandauer Strasse. Cross Karl-Liebknecht-Strasse and turn right to Marx-Engels-Forum.

8 Leave the square between the Konzerthaus (Concert Hall) and the Französischer Dom. Go right onto Charlottenstrasse. Cross the road and continue to rejoin Französische Strasse, turn left. At the traffic lights turn right into Friedrichstrasse (▷ 61), go back to Unter den Linden and the Brandenburger Tor.

7 Soon after Werderscher Strasse becomes Französische Strasse, turn left into Markgrafenstrasse and cross into Gendarmenmarkt (▷ 62–63).

6 Head west along Werderscher Markt toward the twin towers of the Friedrichswerdersche Kirche (▷ 82).

5 Walk to the Nikolaikirche (▷ 80). Turn right onto Propststrasse and continue to the river. Turn right towards the Berliner Dom, then left onto Rathausstrasse and cross the bridge.

ALEXANDERPLATZ WALK

Shopping

ERZGEBIRGSKUNST ORIGINAL

Traditional handmade Christmas decorations beautifully crafted from wood.

✚ L4 ✉ Sophienstrasse 9 ☎ 030 28 26 754 🚇 U-Bahn Weinmeisterstrasse

HACKESCHE HÖFE

Smartened up and commercialized, these historic courtyards remain at the forefront of Berlin's contemporary art scene with art galleries, workshops and cafés.

✚ L4 ✉ Rosenthaler Strasse 40–41 ☎ 030 28 09 80 10 🚇 S-Bahn Hackescher Markt

NIX

A sophisticated range of fashion clothing is sold here for men, women and children.

✚ K4 ✉ Heckmann Höfe, Oranienburger Strasse 32 ☎ 030 281 80 44 🚇 S-Bahn Oranienburger Strasse

RESPECTMEN

Trendy fashions for men by young designers from all over Europe.

✚ L4 ✉ Neue Schönhauser-strasse 14 ☎ 030 28 35 010 🚇 U-Bahn Weinmeisterstrasse

STERLING GOLD

This shop has a range of glamorous evening, ball,

and cocktail wear from the 1950s to the 1980s, and its own dressmaker, who can transform any dress into a perfect fit.

✚ K4 ✉ Heckmann Höfe, Oranienburger Strasse 32 ☎ 030 28 09 65 00 🚇 S-Bahn Oranienburger Strasse

STOFFWECHSEL

You'll find a vast array of funky and fashionable labels such as Miss Sixty, Firetrap, Only, G-Star and Energie—all you'll ever need to look your best.

✚ K4 ✉ Oranienburger Strasse 12 ☎ 030 28 87 96 33 🚇 S-Bahn Hackescher Markt

Entertainment and Nightlife

B-FLAT

Listen to acoustic music and jazz at this downtown club, specially designed for this genre of music; and plenty of big names from the jazz world. Drinks are cheaper before 10pm and happy hour is 1am–2am.

✚ L3 ✉ Rosenthaler Strasse 13 ☎ 030 283 31 23 🚇 U-Bahn Weinmeisterstrasse

CHAMÄLEON

A variety theater that puts on experimental, hard-to-categorize fusion shows—music, dance, comedy, mime, acrobatics, and more—that

are suited even to non-German speakers.

✚ L4 ✉ Hackesche Höfe, Rosenthaler Strasse 40–41 ☎ 030 400 05 90 🚇 S-Bahn Hackescher Markt

KAFFEE BURGER

Expect anything from

poetry slams and samba nights to Balkan discos and live rock at this long-standing alternative club/venue.

✚ L4 ✉ Torstrasse 60 ☎ 030 2804 64 95 🕐 Daily 9pm–late 🚇 U-Bahn Rosa-Luxemburg-Platz

PONY BAR

The interior design of this popular bar may be inspired by the 1960s and 1970s, but the music spun here by weekend DJs is bang up-to-date.

✚ L4 ✉ Alte Schönhauser Strasse 44 🕐 Mon–Sat 12–late, Sun 6pm–late 🚇 U-Bahn Rosa-Luxemburg-Platz

MUSIC FOR ALL

Musical tastes have splintered remarkably in recent years; in Berlin this is evident from the plethora of specialist nightclubs with bebop, house, soul, jungle, ragga, techno and heavy metal—pay your money and take your choice.

Restaurants

PRICES

Prices are approximate, based on a 3-course meal for one person.
€€€ over €40
€€ €20–€40
€ up to €20

CAFÉ BRAVO (€€)

The two cube-shape areas, with mirrored walls and transparent ceilings, form an unusual meeting and eating space in the Kunst-Werke institute. ⊞ K4 ✉ Auguststrasse 69 ☎ 030 23 45 77 77 🕐 Mon–Wed, Fri–Sat 9am–8pm, Thu 9am–9pm, Sun 10am–8pm 🚇 U-Bahn Oranienburger Tor

GAMBRINUS (€)

In a setting of old Berlin photographs and knick-knacks, this local *Kneipe* revels in hearty menu items like *Stolzer Heinrich* (sausage in a beer sauce). ⊞ K4 ✉ Linienstrasse 133 ☎ 030 282 60 43 🕐 Sun–Thu 12–12, Fri–Sat noon–4am 🚇 U-Bahn Oranienburger Tor

HACKESCHER HOF (€€)

A restaurant-café-wine bar with an old-fashioned appeal and an up-to-the-minute menu and style rings the changes on continental cuisine. ⊞ L4 ✉ Rosenthaler Strasse 40–41 ☎ 030 283 52 93 🕐 Mon–Fri 8am–3am, Sat–Sun 9am–3am 🚇 S-Bahn Hackescher Markt

MIRCHI (€€)

Good food is guaranteed at this Indian and Singaporean fusion restaurant and cocktail bar in Mitte. The lunch menu offers vegetarian, chicken and lamb dishes. ⊞ K4 ✉ Oranienburger Strasse 50 ☎ 030 28 44 44 82 🕐 Daily noon–1am 🚇 U-Bahn Oranienburger Tor

MONSIEUR VUONG (€)

Delicious Vietnamese dishes are served at this popular café. It's great value for money. ⊞ L4 ✉ Alte Schönhauser Strasse 46 ☎ 030 99 29 69 24 🕐 Mon–Thu 12–11pm, Fri–Sun 12–midnight 🚇 U-Bahn Weinmeisterstrasse

OSSENA (€–€€)

Visitors and locals alike return again and again to Ossena for the warm welcome and surroundings, prompt service and excellent Italian food at affordable prices. ⊞ L4 ✉ Rosenthaler Strasse 42 ☎ 030 280 998 77 🕐 9am–midnight 🚇 S-Bahn Hackescher Markt

BREAKFAST IN BERLIN

For Berliners, breakfast is a way of life. You can, it seems, take the meal at any time of the day, and you can spend as long over it as you like. Ham and eggs, sausage, cheese, muesli, pumpernickel and even cakes may be on the menu.

OXYMORON (€€)

Find delicious Italian and French food at this 1920s-style lounge in Hackesche Höfe; also a stylish bar and dance floor. ⊞ L4 ✉ Hackesche Höfe, Rosenthaler Strasse 40–41 ☎ 030 28 39 18 86 🕐 Daily 8am–late 🚇 S-Bahn Hackescher Markt

SIXTIES (€)

Red, white and blue are the signature colors of this 1960s American diner-style eatery that rustles up some pretty decent burgers and fries, steaks, shakes, Tex-Mex tacos and more. ⊞ K4 ✉ Oranienburger Strasse 11 ☎ 030 28 59 90 41 🕐 Sun–Thu 10am–2am, Fri–Sat 10am–4am 🚇 S-Bahn Hackescher Markt

TRATTORIA PIAZZA ROSSA (€€)

Smartly dressed folk meet at this eatery in the modern Rathaus Passagen across from the Fernsehturm, for decent Italian fish and meat dishes, and a range of pizzas. ⊞ L5 ✉ Rathausstrasse 13 ☎ 030 612 24 29 🕐 Daily 11am–midnight 🚇 U- and S-Bahn Alexanderplatz

ZUM NUSSBAUM (€)

A traditional Berlin Gasthaus in Nikolaiviertel, artfully designed to look like a 16th-century tavern. ⊞ L5 ✉ Am Nussbaum 3 ☎ 030 242 30 95 🕐 Daily 12–12 🚇 U-Bahn Klosterstrasse

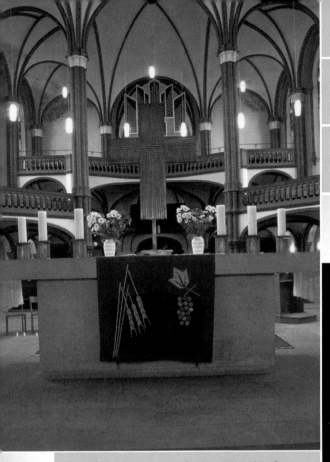

Gentrification proceeds apace in this former East Berlin district, popular with students and ethnic minorities attracted by its low-cost housing, new bars, budget restaurants boutiques, and entertainment venues.

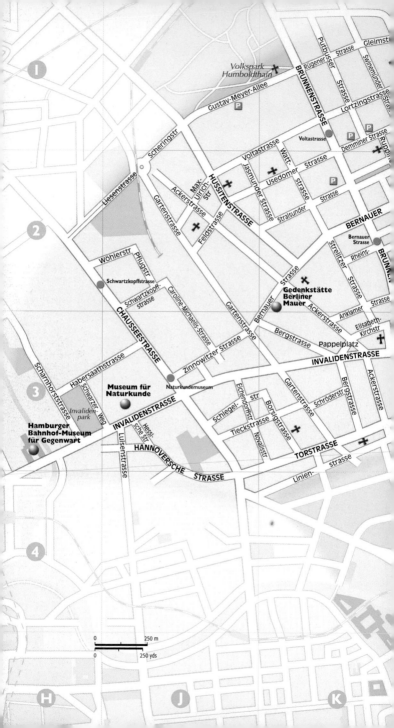

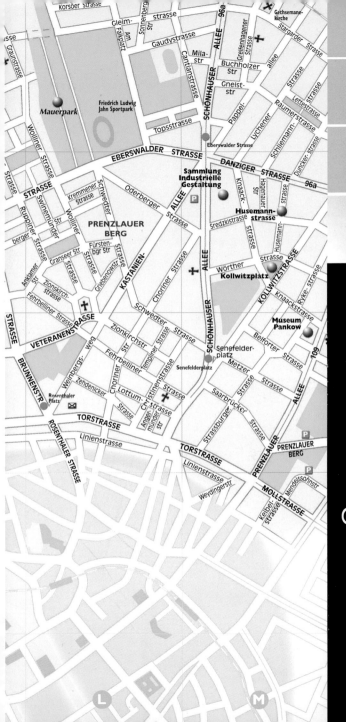

Korsöer Strasse
Gleim-
Falkplatz
Am
Sonnenberger
strasse
Gaudystrasse
Mila-
str
Cantianstrasse
96a
Greifenhagener
Strasse
Gethsemane-
kirche
Stargarder Strasse
Buchholzer
Str
allee
Gneist-
str
Pappel-
Raumerstrasse
Lychener
Schliemann-
Duncker-
strasse
Lettestrasse
Mauerpark
Friedrich Ludwig
Jahn Sportpark
Topsstrasse
Eberswalder Strasse
EBERSWALDER STRASSE
DANZIGER STRASSE
96a
Sammlung
Industrielle
Gestaltung
Knaack-
Str
Hagenauer
STRASSE
Kremmener
Strasse
Schwedter
Oderberger
ALLEE
Husemann-
strasse
Husemann-
Swinemünder
Wolliner
Strasse
Sredzkistrasse
strasse
Strasse
Strasse
PRENZLAUER
BERG
KASTANIEN-
Choriner
Strasse
Strasse
Wörther
Strasse
KOLLWITZSTRASSE
Pyke-strasse
Fürsten-
bgr Str
Granseer Str
Greifenowstr
Strasse
ALLEE
Kollwitzplatz
Knaackstrasse
berger Strasse
Anklamer
str
Zionskirch-
strasse
Schwedter
Strasse
SCHÖNHAUSER
Museum
Pankow
109
STRASSE
Fehrbelliner Strasse
VETERANENSTRASSE
Zionkirchstr
Fehrbelliner
Templiner Strasse
Strasse
Belforter
Strasse
Senefelder-
platz
Metzer
Strasse
BRUNNENSTR
Weinbergs-
weg
Choriner
Zehdenicker
Lottum-
Strasse
Christinenstrasse
Anger-
münder
str
Senefelderplatz
Saarbrücker
Strasse
Strasse
Strassburger
PRENZLAUER
ALLEE
Rosenthaler
Platz
TORSTRASSE
Linienstrasse
TORSTRASSE
PRENZLAUER
BERG
ROSENTHALER STRASSE
Linienstrasse
Weydingerstr
MOLLSTRASSE
Kelbel-
strasse
Mendelsohnstr

L   M

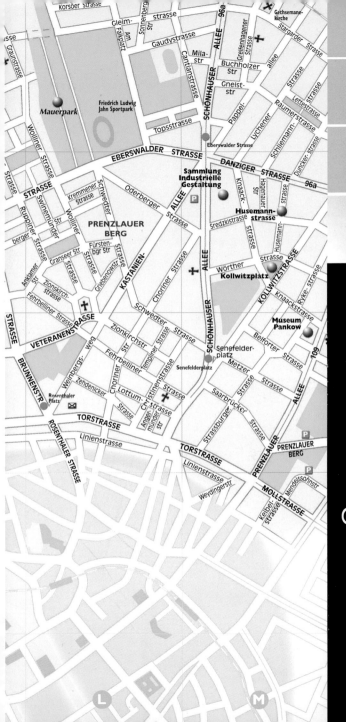

Prenzlauer Berg

Husemannstrasse

 TOP 25

Cafés have sprung up along the charming, wide, tree-lined Husemannstrasse

THE BASICS

🚇 M2
✉ Prenzlauer Berg
🚉 U-Bahn Eberswalder Strasse
🚊 Tram M1, M10, M12
🍴 Many ethnic restaurants and cafés

HIGHLIGHTS

● KulturBrauerei (▷ 93, panel)
● Sammlung Industrielle Gestaltung (▷ 92)

Lying just north of Kollwitzplatz, this short street is typical of the transformation that Prenzlauer Berg has undergone as gentrification of the district continues.

Cultured place Husemannstrasse stands at the heart of the action in Prenzlauer Berg, where trendy shops and cafés are taking over the ground floor areas of renovated postwar apartment blocks. Among the small-scale cultural foundations in this area are the Theater o.N. (Zinnober), founded as the first free theater of the German Democratic Republic (Kollwitzstrasse 53), and the Prater/Volksbühne theater in Kastanienallee. However, the undoubted star of the show is the KulturBrauerei (▷ 93), a multifunctional cultural complex that occupies the handsome buildings of a massive former brewery, and which attracts alternatives-seeking multitudes from around Berlin. In this foundation are theaters, performance and practice venues for alternative music and theater groups, a cinema multiplex, restaurants, and the antique commercial design collection of the Sammlung Industrielle Gestaltung (▷ 92).

Going north At the north end of Husemannstrasse, Danziger Strasse connects with the busy traffic intersection outside the Eberswalder Strasse U-Bahn station, where several tram lines also converge. This is on the way to more residential north Prenzlauer Berg and Pankow, and to the sports facilities at the Friedrich-Ludwig-Jahn-Sportpark. Here, the Max-Schmeling-Halle is used for exhibitions and conventions.

Kollwitzplatz

Now part of a thriving area, Kollwitzplatz is a meeting place for young and old

Named after the artist Käthe Kollwitz (1867–1945), this square in Prenzlauer Berg stands at the heart of a district that has blossomed in recent years. Formerly a rundown part of Communist East Berlin, it has discovered capitalism in a big way.

Mixed images Students, artists and young urban professionals have flocked to Prenzlauer Berg. The district's buildings are a curious mixture: There are a few surviving preWorld War II houses and apartment blocks, some of them still riddled with bullet and shrapnel holes from the Battle of Berlin in 1945; rather more unreconstructed Communist-era edifices, gloomy and shabby-looking, and badly in need of some tender loving care and a lick of paint; and a large stock of brightly painted buildings that have been renovated or rebuilt since the city's reunification. Many renovated buildings can be found in and around Kollwitzplatz.

Jewish character South of Kollwitzplatz, in Rykestrasse, stands the Jüdische Schule (1904), a large former Jewish school, which now houses a synagogue and a Jewish educational foundation. Nearby, the grounds of what was once a Jewish cemetery have been taken over by a playground and a new housing and office development. Across the way, a massive Wasserturm (water tower) in a small park is a signature image of the area. Close to the point where Knaackstrasse emerges into Prenzlauer Allee is the Museum Pankow (▷ 92).

THE BASICS

🚌 M2
✉ Prenzlauer Berg
🚇 U-Bahn Eberswalder Strasse, Senefelderplatz
🚊 Tram M1, M10, M12
🍴 Many ethnic restaurants and cafés

HIGHLIGHTS

● Jüdische Schule
● Wasserturm
● Knaackstrasse
● Museum Pankow (▷ 92)

PRENZLAUER BERG TOP 25

More to See

GEDENKSTÄTTE BERLINER MAUER
www.berliner-mauer-gedenkstaette.de
A section of the Berlin Wall serves as a memorial to those who died, with a Documentation Center and a chapel.
K2 🖂 Bernauer Strasse 111 ☎ 030 467 98 66 66 ⏰ Apr–Oct Tue–Sun 9.30–7; Nov–Mar Tue–Sun 9.30–6 🚇 Nordbahnhof 💷 Free

HAMBURGER BAHNHOF-MUSEUM FÜR GEGENWART
www.smb.museum
This old station has been converted into a gallery of contemporary art.
H3 🖂 Invalidenstrasse 50–51 ☎ 030 39 78 34 12 ⏰ Tue–Fri 10–6, Sat 11–6, Sun 11–6 🚇 S-Bahn Hauptbahnhof, Lehrter Bahnhof 💷 Moderate

MAUERPARK
www.mauerpark.info
This section of the former death strip of the Berlin Wall documents Berlin's history since that time.
L1 🖂 Eberswalder Strasse 🚇 U-Bahn Eberswalder Strasse 🚊 Tram M10

MUSEUM FÜR NATURKUNDE (NATURAL HISTORY MUSEUM)
www.naturkundemuseum-berlin.de
Among geology, palaeontology and zoology exhibits, there's also the world's largest dinosaur skeleton.
J3 🖂 Invalidenstrasse 43 ☎ 030 20 93 85 91 ⏰ Tue–Fri 9.30–6, Sat–Sun 10–6 🚇 U-Bahn Zinnowitzer Strasse 💷 Moderate

MUSEUM PANKOW
This local museum focuses on life here between 1949 and 1990.
M3 🖂 Prenzlauer Allee 227–228 ☎ 030 902 95 39 17 ⏰ Mon–Fri 9–7 🚇 U-Bahn Senefelderplatz 🚊 Tram M2 💷 Free

SAMMLUNG INDUSTRIELLE GESTALTUNG
www.hdg.de
Showing East German design, from the 1950s to the present day.
M2 🖂 Knaackstrasse 97 ☎ 030 473 77 79 40 ⏰ Tue–Fri 9–7, Sat –Sun 10–6 🚇 U-Bahn Eberswalder Strasse 💷 Inexpensive

Graffiti-sprayed murals cover this former death strip of the Berlin Wall

Shopping

EISDIELER

A showcase for up-and-coming Berlin fashion designers, targeting the alternative, young urban and clubbing set.
🚇 L2 ✉ Kastanienallee 12 ☎ 030 28 39 12 91 🚇 U-Bahn Eberswalder Strasse

GURU-LADEN

Everything you need to give your home an exotic facelift. Beautiful printed textiles, Buddhas, banana-leaf notebooks and recycled paper products from India, Nepal, Mexico and Africa.
🚇 M1 ✉ Pappelallee 2

☎ 030 44 01 33 72 🚇 U-Bahn Eberswalder Strasse

JEAN ET LILI

This family business sells beautifully crafted home ware in a Germanically crisp shabby chic style.
🚇 M4 ✉ Winsstrasse 9 ☎ 030 7621 4434 🚇 U-Bahn Senefelderplatz

MR & MRS PEPPERS

The place to shop for authentic 1960s clothing as well as antique clothing, including bathing suits.
🚇 L2 ✉ Kastanienallee 91–92 ☎ 030 448 11 21 🚇 U-Bahn Eberswalder Strasse

SCHALLPLATTEN FRANZ & JOSEF

The friendly staff will help you rifle through the racks of rare vinyl and second-hand CDs. Brand new CDs, too.
🚇 L2 ✉ Kastanienallee 48 ☎ 030 41 71 46 82 🚇 U-Bahn Rosenthaler Platz

VEB ORANGE

Take a trip back to the 1960s and 70s with this trendy collection of fashion and accessories.
🚇 L2 ✉ Oderberger Strasse 29 ☎ 030 97 88 68 86 🚇 U-Bahn Eberswalder Strasse

Entertainment and Nightlife

ALBA BERLIN

If you fancy catching the Albatrosses' skills on the basketball court, head for the O₂ World Arena, one of the best sports venues in the world. There is one midweek and one weekend match per week all year round.
🚇 Off map to east of M6 ✉ Mühlenstrasse 12–30 ☎ 030 300 90 50 🕐 Times vary 🚇 U- or S-Bahn Warschauer Strasse, S-Bahn Ostbahnhof

BADFISH

Highly rated funky bar-hangout with frozen margaritas and a long whisky menu and live music.

🚇 M1 ✉ Stargarerstrasse 13 ☎ 030 54 71 47 88 🕐 Daily 5pm–5am 🚇 S-Bahn Prenzlauer Allee

KESSELHAUS

Enjoy dance nights in a converted former brewery, now known as

---

CULTURAL BREWERY

KulturBrauerei, Schönhauser Allee 36 (tel: 030 44 35 26 14; www.kulturbrauerei-berlin.de), a former brewery in Prenzlauer Berg, is now a multipurpose nightlife, entertainment and dining venue that attracts alternatives-seeking multitudes.

---

the Kultur-Brauerei. This buzzing place accommodates elements of the alternative cultural scene.
🚇 M2 ✉ Knaackstrasse 97 ☎ 030 44 31 50 🕐 Times vary; usually open from 8pm 🚇 U-Bahn Eberswalder Strasse

SODA CLUB

Set in the courtyard of the Kulturbrauerei, this thumping club puts on mainstream party nights for a studenty crowd.
🚇 M2 ✉ Schönhauser Allee 36 ☎ 030 44 31 51 55 🕐 Thu 8–4am, Fri–Sat 11–7am, Sun 7pm–4am; usually open from 7 or 8pm 🚇 U-Bahn Eberswalder Strasse

Restaurants

PRICES

Prices are approximate, based on a 3-course meal for one person.

€€€ over €40
€€ €20–€40
€ up to €20

FRANNZ (€€)

Housed in the vast KulturBrauerei cultural complex, Frannz offers youthful fusion cuisine in a room fitted out in a cool modern style, or on an outside terrace in summer. There's an associated beer garden.
⊞ M2 ✉ Knaackstrasse 97 ☎ 030 72 62 79 360 🕓 Thu–Sun 6pm–late 🚇 U-Bahn Eberswalder Strasse

FRIDA KAHLO (€€)

Mexican restaurant with all its quesadillas, fajitas, enchiladas and burritos firmly in place. The theme pays homage to the early 20th-century Mexican painter of the same name.
⊞ M1 ✉ Lychener Strasse 37 ☎ 030 445 70 16 🕓 Mon–Thu 9am–2am, Fri–Sat 9am–3am 🚇 U-Bahn Eberswalder Strasse

GOLDEN BUDDHA (€)

You'll likely find yourself squeezed convivially into this popular restaurant, or at an outdoor table, for Thai atmosphere and delicate yet inexpensive food.
⊞ M1 ✉ Gleimstrasse 26 ☎ 030 448 55 56 🕓 Mon–Fri 12–12, Sat 1–12 🚇 U- or S-Bahn Schönhauser Allee

KONNOPKE'S IMBISS (€)

Should you be a fan of that Berlin delicacy, *Currywurst* (sausage with a curry-ketchup sauce) with fries, there's no better place than at this world-famous (in Berlin) snackbar underneath the U-Bahn station.
⊞ M2 ✉ Schönhauser Allee 44a ☎ 030 442 77 65 🕓 Mon–Fri 9am–8pm, Sat 12–8 🚇 U-Bahn Eberswalder Strasse

MAO THAI STAMMHAUS (€€)

This is widely regarded as the finest Thai restaurant in Berlin, with top-class service and elegant surroundings. The beautifully presented food deserves its excellent reputation.
⊞ M2 ✉ Wörther Strasse 30 ☎ 030 441 92 61 🕓 Daily 12–11.30pm 🚇 U-Bahn Senefelderplatz

METZER ECK (€)

The Prenzlauer Berg's oldest eatery opened

GOOD VALUE

in 1913 and little has changed since. The traditional fare is pure Berlin and no dish is over €10.
⊞ M3 ✉ Metzer Strasse 33 ☎ 030 442 76 56 🕓 Mon–Sat 4pm–1am 🚇 U-Bahn Senefelderplatz

NEUGRÜNS KÖCHE (€€)

A young and relaxed restaurant with two menus to choose from—Mediterranean or regional—both of which are excellent value.
⊞ M1 ✉ Schönhauser Allee 135a ☎ 030 44 01 20 92 🕓 Mon–Sat from 6pm 🚇 U-Bahn Eberswalder Strasse

PASTERNAK (€€)

Marina Lehmann's lovely restaurant, which serves a wide range of traditional Russian fare, has a literary theme. It is extremely popular with local people.
⊞ M2 ✉ Knaackstrasse 22–24 ☎ 030 441 33 99 🕓 Daily 9am–1am 🚇 U-Bahn Senefelderplatz

WEINSTEIN (€€)

Weinstein is a wine bar, bistro and restaurant reminiscent of Paris restaurants in the late 19th and early 20th centuries. There's classic German and French food and a quality wine list.
⊞ M1 ✉ Lychener Strasse 33 ☎ 030 441 18 42 🕓 Mon–Sat 5pm–2am, Sun 6pm–2am 🚇 U-Bahn Eberswalder Strasse

Berliners are spoiled for choice when it's time to get away from the stresses of city life. Right on their doorstep there are parks, forests, lakes and pretty villages that are much-loved places of escape.

Sights	98–106	Top 25	**TOP 25**

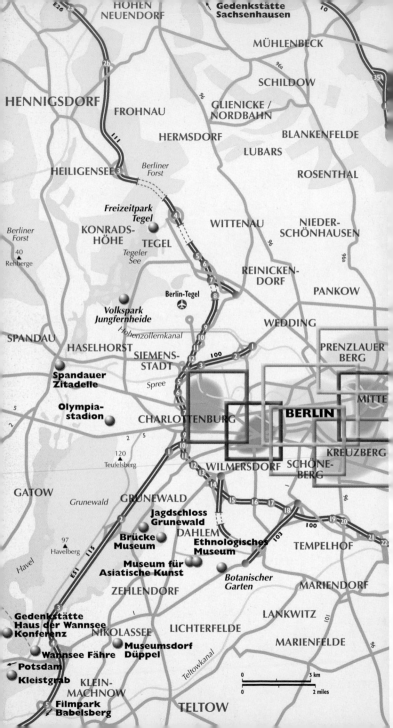

BERNAU

ZEPERNICK

BUCH

16

FRANZÖSISCH
BUCHHOLZ

KAROW

SCHWANEBECK

ESS

109

ESS

10

17

71
Peckberge

158

ESS

158

E28

2

BLANKENBURG

MALCHOW

WARTENBERG

WEISSENSEE

HOHEN-
SCHÖNHAUSEN

MARZAHN

HÖNOW

**Zeiss-
Grossplanetarium**

LICHTENBERG

FRIEDRICHS-
HAIN

1   5

KAULSDORF

**East Side
Gallery**

FRIEDRICHS-
FELDE

BIESDORF

Oberbaumbrücke

*Tierpark
Berlin*

KARLSHORST

NEUKÖLLN

*Treptower
Park*

BAUMSCHULENWEG

25

FRIEDRICHS-
HAGEN

23

24

96a

2

JOHANNISTHAL

KÖPENICK

*Grosser
Müggelsee*

BRITZ

3

113

**Schloss
Köpenick**

*Britzer
Garten*

Teltowkanal

4

E36

Dahme

179

5

GRÜNAU

BUCKOW

RUDOW

ALT-
GLIENICKE

LICHTENRADE

6

BOHNSDORF

7

Ethnologisches Museum

Exhibits at the Ethnological Museum (right) include detailed Mayan carvings (left)

THE BASICS

www.smb.museum
🔼 Off map to south
✉ Lansstrasse 8, Dahlem
☎ 030 266 42 42 42
🕐 Tue–Fri 10–5, Sat–Sun 11–6
🍴 Café
Ⓤ U-Bahn Dahlem-Dorf
🚌 110, X83, X11
♿ Good
👖 Inexpensive

HIGHLIGHTS

● Polynesian clubhouse
● Oceanian boats
● Pre-Columbian gold statuettes
● Peruvian pottery
● Throne and footstool from Cameroon
● Benin bronzes
● Indonesian shadow puppets
● Sri Lankan carved masks
● Australian bark painting
● World music headphones

The folk art theme extends beyond the Ethnological Museum to the nearby Dahlem-Dorf U-Bahn station, where modern primitivist sculptures offer provocative seating. Test them for comfort, then make your own artistic judgment.

Exhibitions Although the airy rooms of the Ethnologisches Museum appear large, there is exhibition space for only a fraction of its 400,000-plus ethnological items. Still, the Americas, Oceania, Africa, East Asia and South Asia are all represented by permanent exhibitions, backed up by temporary displays.

Oceania The Oceanian boats are probably the highlight of the collection. The display includes an 18th-century vessel known as a Tongiaki from Tonga, which resembles a catamaran. For landlubbers there is the fantastically decorated male clubhouse, from the Palau Islands of the western Pacific.

Pre-Columbian art The focus of the American collection is the exhibition of ancient sculptures and figurines, mainly originating from Mexico and Peru. Gold was the medium preferred by many of these artists and the craftsmanship represented here is perhaps among the best of its kind in the world. Just as beautiful, and more arresting, are the decorated stone *stelae* from Cozumalhuapa (Guatemala), which were created to fend off evil spirits.

This Renaissance-style hunting lodge has been used for more than 400 years

TOP 25

Jagdschloss Grunewald

The Grunewald forest is an amazing woodland on the western edge of Berlin. The dreamily scenic 32sq km (12sq miles), dotted with lakes, beaches and nature reserves, are the preferred playground of Berliners at weekends.

Hunting lodge Jagdschloss Grunewald is an attractive Renaissance hunting lodge, built in 1542 for Elector Joachim II of Brandenburg. The stables and outbuildings date from around 1700, when the house was surrounded by a moat. Today the lodge is a museum decorated with paintings and furniture from various royal collections; the chase is the predominant theme. One picture shows Kaiser Wilhelm II on a visit to the Grunewald. The 17th-century Dutch school is well represented among the paintings, but the best work is by a German, Lucas Cranach the Elder. Equally remarkable is the painted wooden ceiling of the Great Hall (Grosser Saal) on the ground floor. The schloss was untouched during World War II and is Berlin's oldest surviving castle.

Grunewald forest Paths crisscross the forest, beaches fringe the Havel and there is space for leisure pursuits from boating to hang-gliding. You can swim in the Grunewaldsee, the lake on which the hunting lodge stands, and, farther south, in the Krumme Lanke. Between these two lakes is a marshy nature reserve known as the Langes Luch. For views, climb the Grunewaldturm, a 72m (236ft) folly on the banks of the Havel, built in memory of Kaiser Wilhelm I in 1897.

THE BASICS

Jagdschloss Grunewald

www.spsg.de

➕ Off map to southwest

✉ Hüttenweg 100, Am Grunewaldsee

☎ 030 813 35 97

🕐 Apr–Oct Tue–Sun 10–6; Nov–Mar Sat–Sun 10–4

🚆 S-Bahn Grunewald

🚌 M19, M29, X10, 115, 186, 249, 349

✋ Inexpensive

Grunewaldturm

➕ Off map to southwest

✉ Havelchaussee 61, Wilmersdorf

☎ 030 300 07 30

🕐 Tower: daily 10–6 (10am–midnight in summer)

🍴 Restaurant

🚆 S-Bahn Grunewald

🚌 218

✋ Inexpensive

HIGHLIGHTS

Jagdschloss Grunewald

● Hunting museum

● *Adam and Eve and Judith,* Lucas Cranach the Elder

● *Julius Caesar,* Rubens

● Wooden ceiling in the Great Hall

FARTHER AFIELD TOP 25

Spandauer Zitadelle

The 16th-century Zitadelle at Spandau (left); Nikolaikirche in the Altstadt (right)

THE BASICS

www.zitadelle-spandau.de
🔲 Off map to west
✉ Am Juliusturm 64, Spandau
☎ 030 354 94 40
🕐 Daily 10–5
🍴 Am Juliusturm, Zitadelle
🚇 U-Bahn Zitadelle
🚌 X33
🚈 Spandau
♿ Few
💷 Inexpensive

HIGHLIGHTS

● Cannons
● Statue of Albrecht the Bear
● Museum of the Middle Ages
● Juliusturm
● Bastion walls
● Old Magazine
● Ruined arsenal
● Kolk

Of the many attractive villages on Berlin's outskirts, ancient Spandau, with its red-brick Zitadelle, picturesque streets and views across the Havel, stands out. The best vantage point is the Juliusturm, the oldest surviving part of the complex.

The Zitadelle A strategic location at the confluence of the rivers Spree and Havel made Spandau important in the Middle Ages. The first Zitadelle (fortress), dating from the 12th century, was rebuilt by Joachim III in 1557. The oldest surviving part of the building is the crenellated Juliusturm—the view from the top of the tower is worth the steep climb. Most of the bastions and outbuildings date from the 19th century, though the Old Magazine is as ancient as the castle itself.

Many lives One exhibit in the museum at Spandau castle is an 1860 cannon, brought back from Siberia, where it had languished for more than a century. The fortress last saw active service during the Napoleonic Wars, when the Old Arsenal was reduced to ruins. Just inside the castle gateway is the statue of a defiant Albrecht, the famous Bear of Brandenburg.

Altstadt Spandau The attractive Old Town is a short walk from the castle. The Gotisches Haus (Gothic House) in Breite Strasse dates from 1232. In Reformationsplatz, the central square, are plenty of cafés and the splendid Gothic church, Nikolaikirche. North of here lies the quaint old area known as the Kolk.

More to See

BOTANISCHER GARTEN (BOTANICAL GARDEN)

www.bgbm.org

See more than 18,000 varieties of plants and flowers in beautifully landscaped grounds.

🔾 Off map to south 🖂 Königin-Luise-Platz 1, Dahlem ☎ 030 83 85 01 00 🕙 May–Jul daily 9–9; Apr, Aug 9–8; Sep 9–7; Mar, Oct 9–6; Feb 9–5; Nov–Jan 9–4 🚇 S-Bahn Botanischer Garten 🖐 Moderate

BRITZER GARTEN

www.gruen-berlin.de

Created for the National Garden Show in 1985, the 100ha (247-acre) site is popular with Berliners. There are nature trails, a lake and a restaurant.

🔾 Off map to southeast 🖂 Sangerhauser Weg 1, Neukölln ☎ 030 700 90 60 🕙 Daily 9–dusk 🚌 179 🖐 Inexpensive

BRÜCKE MUSEUM

www.bruecke-museum.de

This gallery exhibits work from the group of 20th-century German artists known as Die Brücke.

🔾 Off map to southwest 🖂 Bussardsteig 9, Dahlem ☎ 030 831 20 29 🕙 Wed–Mon 11–5 🚌 115 🖐 Moderate

EAST SIDE GALLERY

www.eastsidegallery-berlin.com

See graffiti art as displayed on 730m (2,395ft) of the former Berlin Wall, on the north bank of the River Spree. It is said to be the world's largest open-air art gallery.

🔾 Off map to east 🖂 Mühlenstrasse 🚇 U- and S-Bahn Warschauer Strasse 🖐 Free

FILMPARK BABELSBERG

www.filmpark-babelsberg.de

The hub of Germany's film industry for 90 years, these vast studios were responsible for such classics as *Metropolis* (1927) and *The Blue Angel* (1930). You can enjoy a studio tour and experience the cinema of the future at this popular attraction.

🔾 Off map to southwest
🖂 Grossbeerenstrasse, 14482 Potsdam
☎ 0331 721 27 50 🕙 Mid-Mar–Oct daily 10–6 🖐 Expensive 🚌 601, 619, 690 from Potsdam train station

Adolf Engler's Tropical House at the Botanical Garden

Satirical graffiti at the East Side Gallery

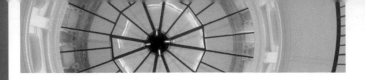

FREIZEITPARK TEGEL

Possibly Berlin's best park, and certainly its best for children, with table tennis, rowing, trampolines, volleyball, pedal boats and chess. Cruises depart from the Greenwich promenade nearby.

➕ Off map to northwest ✉ Campestrasse 11 🕐 May–Sep daily 8–5 (attractions); park 24 hours 🚇 U-Bahn Alt-Tegel

FRIEDRICHSHAGEN

www.friedrichshagen.net

A distinct small town within the big city, this has always been a popular spot at the Müggelsee, Berlin's largest lake. It's especially popular in summer for water sports.

➕ Off map to southeast ✉ Köpenick 🚉 S-Bahn Friedrichshagen 🚊 Tram 60, 61 to Seebad Friedrichshagen

GEDENKSTÄTTE HAUS DER WANNSEE KONFERENZ (CONFERENCE HOUSE MEMORIAL)

www.ghwk.de

In this innocuous-looking mansion beside the shores of the Wannsee lake, leading Nazis plotted the deliberate and systematic mass extermination of Europe's 11 million Jews. The exhibition tells the whole horrific story.

➕ Off map to southwest ✉ Am Grossen Wannsee 56–58, Zehlendorf ☎ 030 805 00 10 🕐 Daily 10–6 🚉 S-Bahn Wannsee ✋ Free

GEDENKSTÄTTE SACHSENHAUSEN

www.stiftung-bg.de

Some 100,000 prisoners perished at this concentration camp during World War II. The great lie "Work makes you free," inscribed on the entrance gate, is a chilling reminder of the deception and evil once perpetrated here. Two museums tell the terrible story of the camp. One focuses on the plight of the Jews; the other, in the former kitchens, focuses on the daily life of the inmates.

➕ Off map to northwest ✉ Strasse der Nationen 22 ☎ 033 01 20 02 00 🕐 Mid-Mar–mid-Oct daily 8.30–6; mid-Oct–mid-Mar

The sign on the gates of Sachsenhausen Concentration Camp gave false hope to all who perished here (above)

Action hero at Filmpark Babelsberg (left; ▷ 101)

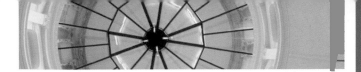

8.30–4.30 🚈 S-Bahn Oranienburg (then 20-minute walk) 🚉 Oranienburg ♿ Few 🎟 Free

KLEISTGRAB (KLEIST'S GRAVE)

Tucked away in a secluded spot in Wannsee is the grave of the Romantic poet Heinrich von Kleist, who committed suicide here with his mistress in 1811.

➕ Off map to southwest ✉ Bismarckstrasse, Zehlendorf 🚈 S-Bahn Wannsee

MUSEUM FÜR ASIATISCHE KUNST (MUSEUM OF ASIAN ART)

www.smb.museum

The art and culture of the Indian sub-continent and Asia is displayed here.

➕ Off map to south ✉ Lansstrasse 8 ☎ 030 266 42 42 42 🕐 Tue–Fri 10–5, Sat–Sun 11–6 🚈 U-Bahn Dahlem-Dorf 🎟 Inexpensive

MUSEUMSDORF DÜPPEL

www.dueppel.de

On the site of a village founded around 1170, this open-air living museum is a re-creation of a medieval village. Costumed re-enactors afford visitors an insight into life in the Berlin area during the Middle Ages and display some of the arts, crafts and household activities of the period.

➕ Off map to southwest ✉ Clauerstrasse 11, Zehlendorf ☎ 030 802 66 71 🕐 Sun and hols 10–5, Thu 3–7 🚈 S-Bahn Mexikoplatz, then bus 118 🎟 Inexpensive

OBERBAUMBRÜCKE

More than 500 different kinds of tiles were used in the renovation of what was once Berlin's longest bridge.

➕ Off map to east ✉ Mühlenstrasse 🚈 U-Bahn Schlesisches Tor

OLYMPIASTADION (OLYMPIC STADIUM)

www.olympiastadion-berlin.de

This famous stadium was built to host the 1936 Olympics, and was renovated as the venue for the 2006 soccer world cup final.

➕ Off map to west ✉ Olympischer Platz 3 ☎ 030 25 00 23 22 (information) 🚈 U- and S-Bahn Olympiastadion 🎟 Inexpensive

The Oberbaumbrücke is an imposing sight

More to See in and around Potsdam

ALTER MARKT

The Old Market is the hub of Potsdam, with the Nikolaikirche at its heart. Crown Prince Friedrich Wilhelm IV commissioned the building but he had to wait until after his father died before completing the project and adding the distinguished dome to the roof. The 18th-century baroque Altes Rathaus (Old City Hall), adorned with a gilded figure of Atlas, forms part of Potsdam's city walls. Framing the remaining sides of the market square are a large 1970s structure and parts of the Stadtschloss (City Castle), which was badly damaged during World War II and then demolished by city planners in 1959.

➕ Off map to southwest ✉ Am Alten Markt 🚇 S-Bahn Potsdam Hauptbahnhof 🚋 Tram X98, 91, 92, 93, 96, 99

SANSSOUCI

www.spsg.de

On the western edge of Potsdam you'll find landscaped Sanssouci Park. It contains two quite different yet equally impressive palaces built for Frederick the Great. Formal gardens, terraces lined with fruit trees, fountains and follies complete the picture. Schloss Sanssouci was designed by Georg Wenzeslaus von Knobelsdorff. The single-story rococo facade, topped by a shallow green dome, conceals a succession of gorgeously furnished rooms and a charming collection of precious objects. The best view of the expansive redbrick facade of the New Palace (Neues Palais) is to be had from the imposing driveway. Johann Büring designed the facade, and Karl von Gontard the sumptuous interior. About a dozen of the palace's more than 200 rooms are open to visitors.

➕ Off map to southwest ✉ Maulbeerallee, Potsdam ☎ 0331 969 42 00 🕐 Schloss: Apr–Oct Tue–Sun 10–6; Nov–Mar Tue–Sun 10–5; Neues Palais: Apr–Oct Tue–Sun 10–6; Nov–Mar Tue–Sun 10–5 🍴 Café; restaurant 🚇 S-Bahn Potsdam Hauptbahnhof 🚌 695, X15 🚉 Wild Park 🦽 Few 🖐 Park: free; Schloss: expensive; Neues Palais: moderate

Sumptuous Schloss Sanssouci has fine rococo detail and lavishly furnished rooms

SCHLOSS CECILIENHOF

www.spsg.de

North of Potsdam, set in parkland, is Schloss Cecilienhof, built for Crown Prince Wilhelm, Kaiser Wilhelm II's son. Completed in 1917, it is an early 20th-century reproduction of a half-timber English Tudor manor house. In the summer of 1945, Cecilienhof was the setting for the Potsdam Conference, when US President Harry S. Truman, Soviet political leader Joseph Stalin and British Prime Minister Winston Churchill met to shape the fate of the postwar world. Cecilienhof is now a luxury hotel.

🛨 Off map to southwest ✉ Im Neuen Garten 11 ☎ 0331 969 42 00 🕓 Apr–Oct Tue–Sun 10–6; Nov–Mar Tue–Sun 10–5 🍴 Restaurant 🚇 S-Bahn Potsdam Hauptbahnhof 🚌 692 💷 Moderate

SCHLOSS GLIENICKE

www.spsg.de

The mock-Renaissance schloss was designed in 1824 by Karl Friedrich Schinkel for Prince Friedrich Karl of Prussia, brother of Kaiser Wilhelm I.

Nowadays the grounds are known for their arcadian follies and ornamental garden. The follies are by Schinkel, and the park was laid out by Peter Lenné, also responsible for Berlin's Tiergarten. Echoes of Renaissance Italy and Classical Greece can be detected among the follies. The most extraordinary flight of fancy must be the Klosterhof, with genuine remains from Venice and Pisa. Just outside the gate is Glienicker Brücke. The bridge came to the world's attention in 1962 when, marking the border between East and West, it was the scene of a swap involving the US pilot Gary Powers, who had been shot down by the Soviet air force on allegations of spying. The bridge subsequently starred in films and became a symbol of the Cold War.

🛨 Off map to southwest ✉ Königstrasse 36 ☎ 0331 969 42 00 🕓 Park: daily 7am–8pm. Schloss: Apr–Oct Tue–Sun 10–6; Nov–Mar Sat–Sun 10–5 (guided tours only) 🍴 Excellent restaurant 🚇 S-Bahn Wannsee, then bus 316 🚋 Tram 93 from Potsdam 💷 Inexpensive

Schloss Cecilienhof is a touch of England in a foreign land

More to See

SCHLOSS KÖPENICK
www.smb.museum
Standing in peaceful parkland, this elegant 17th-century palace houses a museum of decorative arts.
✚ Off map to southeast ✉ Schlossinsel, Köpenick ☎ 030 65 66 17 48 🕐 Tue–Sun 11–6 🍴 Café 🚇 S-Bahn Spindlersfeld 🚌 164, 167; tram 27, 60, 61, 62, 67 👋 Inexpensive

TIERPARK BERLIN
One of Berlin's two zoos, on the east side of the city in grounds that once formed part of Schloss Friedrichsfelde. Events are held in the restored palace.
✚ Off map to east ✉ Am Tierpark 125 ☎ 030 51 53 10 🕐 Jan–mid Mar and Nov–Dec daily 9–4; mid-Sep–Oct daily 9–5; mid-Mar–mid-Sep daily 9–6 🚇 U-Bahn Tierpark 🚌 296, 396; tram 27, 37 👋 Expensive

TREPTOWER PARK
The largest green space on the eastern side of the city spreads out along the banks of the River Spree. Fairs and other events are often held here.
✚ Off map to east ✉ Puschkinallee 🚇 S-Bahn Treptower Park

VOLKSPARK JUNGFERNHEIDE
This large park, on the northern edge of Charlottenburg, offers swimming, boat rental, hiking, sports fields and a theater.
✚ Off map to northwest ✉ Saatwinkler Damm 🚇 U-Bahn Jakob-Kaiser-Platz

WANNSEE FÄHRE
The enjoyable ferry ride from Wannsee to Kladow is inexpensive (free with a *Tageskarte*).
✚ Off map to southwest ✉ Wannsee Pier ⛴ Ferry F10 🚇 U-Bahn Wannsee

ZEISS-GROSSPLANETARIUM
www.sdtb.de
Built during the 1980s to match a planetarium in West Berlin, you'll find the latest optical and laser technology for its astronomy shows here.
✚ Off map east of M1 ✉ Prenzlauer Allee 80 ☎ 030 421 84 50 🕐 Shows daily 2 and 4pm and varying additional times 🚇 S-Bahn Prenzlauer Allee 👋 Moderate

Treptower Park is a great place to relax and glimpse the city

Berlin caters to all, having a good selection of budget, mid-range and luxury hotels, as well as inexpensive hostels. If you're looking for a good-quality hotel, it's usually best to reserve a room in advance.

Where to Stay

Introduction

The steadily increasing number of visitors to Berlin has brought rapid growth and investment in the city's hotel industry, mainly in the luxury market. Good-quality mid-range and budget hotels tend to book up fast, but there is also an excellent selection of well-equipped hostels.

Location, Location

Budget hotels can be found virtually all over, with particular concentrations around Hackescher Markt, the lower end of Friedrichstrasse, Prenzlauer Berg, Kreuzberg, Friedrichsfelde, and parts of Charlottenburg and Wilmersdorf. They tend to be on side streets, but are never far from public transportation. Mid-range hotels cluster around Kurfürstendamm, Charlottenburg, Schöneberg and the top end of Friedrichstrasse. Luxury hotels and business hotels are to be found around Unter den Linden, Kurfürstendamm, Savignyplatz and the middle section of Friedrichstrasse. Scenic, leafy outer locations include Wannsee, Grunewald and Müggelsee. Good transportation ensures quick transfers.

Breakfast Specials

Most hotels have a breakfast buffet, which can be simply *Kaffee und Schrippen* (coffee and rolls) with cheese and cold meats, or a feast of smoked meats, fresh fruit and cake. Breakfast is often not included in the price of a room in luxury and mid-range hotels, but is included in budget hotels and hostels.

FINDING A ROOM

Rooms can be booked in advance through the Berlin tourism website www.visitberlin.de or through the hotel finder at www.germany-tourism.de. The best place to start your search once you are in the city is at the nearest tourist office, which offers a room-reservation service for a charge of €3 (free for phone bookings; tel 030 25 00 23 33). If the tourist office is closed just take a stroll round the middle of town.

Berlin caters to all accommodations needs, from simple hotels to grand, luxury establishments

Budget Hotels

A & O FRIEDRICHSHAIN

www.aohostels.com
Inexpensive rooms in the old east end. Multilingual staff, cut-price meals and bike rental. Families are well catered for.
✚ Off map to east
✉ Boxhagener Strasse 73
☎ 030 809 47 54 00
Ⓢ S-Bahn Ostkreuz

BERLINER CITY-PENSION

www.berliner-city-pension.de
In the heart of Mitte in Alexanderplatz. Rooms in this renovated hotel are clean and light.
✚ Off map to east ✉ Proskauer Strasse 13 ☎ 030 42 08 16 15
Ⓤ U-Bahn Samariter Strasse

CIRCUS

www.circus-berlin.de
Central hostel popular with backpackers. Luggage store, bike rental, ticket service and 24-hour reception.
✚ L3 ✉ Weinbergsweg 1a
☎ 030 20 00 39 39
Ⓤ U-Bahn Rosenthaler Platz

FRAUENHOTEL ARTEMISIA

www.frauenhotel-berlin.de
Just for women—with 12 attractive rooms, a bar and a library—in Wilmersdorf. Book early to get your space.

✚ B8 ✉ Brandenburgische Strasse 18 ☎ 030 860 93 20
Ⓤ U-Bahn Konstanzer Strasse

HOTEL AM SCHLOSS BELLEVUE

www.hotelamschloss bellevue.de
A family-run hotel in a central yet quiet location not far from Kurfürstendamm.
✚ G4 ✉ Paulstrasse 3
☎ 030 391 12 27 Ⓤ U-Bahn Turmstrasse

HOTEL-PENSION MÜNCHEN

www.hotel-pension-muenchen-in-berlin.de
Modern sculptures and paintings by local artists grace this lodging in the Wilmersdorf district. The artist owner keeps it clean and personable. Room types range from single without bathroom to four-person apartments with en-suite.
✚ E9 ✉ Güntzelstrasse 62
☎ 030 857 91 20 Ⓤ U-Bahn Güntzelstrasse

HOTEL TRANSIT LOFT

www.transit-loft.de
This is one of the best hotels in the lower price range. Transit Loft has 47 clean rooms and surprisingly good facilities.
✚ Off map to northeast
✉ Immanuelkirchstrasse 14a ☎ 030 48 49 37 73
Ⓣ Tram M4

MEININGER BERLIN MITTE

www.meininger-hotels.com
Great value for money, this stylish hotel/hostel has no curfew and offers a huge breakfast.
✚ K4 ✉ Oranienburger Strasse ☎ 030 31 87 98 16
Ⓤ U-Bahn Möckernbrücke, Hallesches Tor

OSTEL

www.ostel.eu
The 16 rooms of this hostel in former East Berlin are a reservoir of "Ostalgie" (nostalgia for the East) and retro-Communist chic.
✚ Off map to east
✉ Wriezener Karree 5
☎ 030 25 76 86 60
Ⓢ S-Bahn Ostbahnhof

PEGASUS HOSTEL

www.hostel-berlin-pegasus.com
This hostel has more to offer than most—a pleasant garden, excellent cooking facilities, apartments and the choice of private or shared showers.
✚ Off map to east ✉ Strasse der Pariser Kommune 35
☎ 030 297 73 60 Ⓤ U-Bahn Weberwiese

Mid-Range Hotels

PRICES

Expect to pay between €100 and €200 for per night for a double room in a mid-range hotel.

ARTE LUISE KUNSTHOTEL

www.luise-berlin.com
Different well-known artists have designed each room in this hotel for art buffs, built in 1825 as a city mansion. It has a striking facade, a lobby filled with sculptures, a large hall for exhibitions, and philosophical maxims decorating the stairway.
✚ J4 ✉ Luisenstrasse 19
☎ 030 28 44 80 Ⓤ U- and S-Bahn Friedrichstrasse

ART'OTEL BERLIN MITTE

www.artotel.de
In this designer hotel are paintings by artist Georg Baselitz (*b.*1938), along with a choice of red, green, blue or aubergine room tones, and fusion cuisine in the restaurant.
✚ L6 ✉ Wallstrasse 70–73
✉ 030 24 06 20 Ⓤ U- and S-Bahn Friedrichstrasse

AZIMUT

www.azimuthotels.de
This hotel offers excellent service, clean and spacious rooms and is close to the action just off Kurfürstendamm. The rooftop café terrace is a great spot for admiring the view on a summer's evening.
✚ D7 ✉ Joachimstaler

Strasse 39–40 ✉ 030 88 91 10 Ⓤ U-Bahn Kurfürstendamm

BERLIN MARK HOTEL

www.berlinmarkhotels.de
The 60 high-ceilinged rooms of this hotel just off Kurfürstendamm are decorated in an old-fashioned bourgeois style, with a modern art touch.
✚ D7 ✉ Meinekestrasse 10
☎ 030 97 80 88 88
Ⓤ U-Bahn Kurfürstendamm

CIRCUS

www.circus-berlin.de
Opened in 2008, the Circus puts on quite a performance. It has youthful verve, color and a highly individual, up-to-the-minute designer style, combined with a great quality to price ratio.
✚ L3 ✉ Rosenthaler Strasse 1 ☎ 030 20 00 39 39
Ⓤ U-Bahn Rosenthaler Platz

CAMPING

There are several decent campsites in and around Berlin. A convenient urban site is Tentstation Berlin ✉ Seydlitzstrasse 6 ☎ 030 39 40 46 40; www.tentstation.de Ⓤ U- or S-Bahn Hauptbahnhof), a few blocks northwest of Berlin's main train station. Farther out, on the shore of the Tegeler See, is Zeltplatz Saatwinkel ✉ Maienwerderweg im Jagen 61 ☎ 030 60 97 35 80; www.zeltplatz-saatwinkel.de Ⓔ X33, 133

FJORD HOTEL

www.fjordhotelberlin.de
Clean and modern, this 57-room hotel is convenient for the Kulturforum. A roof terrace is open for breakfast in summer.
✚ H7 ✉ Bissingzeile 13
☎ 030 52 68 54 Ⓤ U-Bahn Mendelssohn-Bartholdy-Park

HANSABLICK

www.hotel-hansablick.de
On a quiet side street beside the Spree, this hotel has warm, small rooms with a slightly chintzy modern style, some with a river view and balcony, in a town house of 1900.
✚ E5 ✉ Flotowstrasse 6
☎ 030 390 48 00 Ⓢ S-Bahn Tiergarten

HONIGMOND GARDEN HOTEL

www.honigmond.de
The main attraction of this small hotel in Scheunenviertel is its beautiful garden and intimate surroundings. You can sit outside during the summer.
✚ J3 ✉ Invalidenstrasse 122
☎ 030 28 44 55 77
Ⓢ S-Bahn Nordbahnhof

HOTEL GATES BERLIN CITY EAST

www.hotel-gates.com
Comfortable and modern 35-room hotel, opposite the Natural History Museum, with a small bar, restaurant and sauna.
✚ J3 ✉ Invalidenstrasse 98
☎ 030 31 10 60 Ⓤ U-Bahn Zinnowitzer Strasse

HOTEL JURINE
www.hotel-jurine.de
This family-run hotel is close to Prenzlauer Berg. All 49 airy rooms have pay and satellite TV.
⊞ L3 ⊠ Schwedter Strasse 15 ☎ 030 443 29 90
🚇 U-Bahn Senefelderplatz

HOTEL KASTANIENHOF
www.kastanienhof.biz
A friendly hotel with *Altberliner Charme* (Old Berlin charm) in a typical 19th-century apartment building. Every room is individually designed.
⊞ L2 ⊠ Kastanienallee 65 ☎ 030 44 30 50 🚇 U-Bahn Rosenthaler Platz

HOTEL-PENSION SAVOY
www.hotel-pension-savoy.de
The Savoy is off to the east in Kurfürstendamm. Each of the 20 guest rooms has modern amenities including cable TV, telephone, hair dryer and safety deposit box, as well as a bathroom with bath or shower. Bicycles to rent.
⊞ D7 ⊠ Meinekestrasse 4 ☎ 030 88 47 16 10
🚇 U-Bahn Kurfürstendamm

HOTEL RIEHMERS HOFGARTEN
www.riehmers-hofgarten.de
This florid stucco apartment house was built in 1891 for wealthy Berliners; and has 20 good-size rooms.
⊞ J8 ⊠ Yorckstrasse 83 ☎ 030 78 09 88 00
🚇 U-Bahn Mehringdamm

HOTEL VILLA KASTANIA
www.villakastania.de
Comfortable hotel in Charlottenburg. The 47 rooms have good facilities, and there is a pool.
⊞ Off map to west ⊠ Kastanienallee 20 ☎ 030 30 000 20 🚇 U-Bahn Theodor-Heuss-Platz

LUISENHOF
www.luisenhof.de
Built in 1822, the graceful Luisenhof manages to be both close to the heart of the action in Mitte and tranquil at the same time. The rooms are bright and modern yet still retain an element of the house's original character.
⊞ M6 ⊠ Köpenicker Strasse 92 ☎ 030 246 28 10 🚇 U-Bahn Märkisches Museum

NH BERLIN-KURFÜRSTENDAMM
www.nh-hotels.com
No-nonsense business hotel with immaculate

WHERE TO LOOK

Berlin offers a surprising variety of lower-priced accommodations and you do not necessarily need to trek out to the backwoods. Schöneberg and Kreuzberg districts both have a plentiful supply of pensions and simple hotels, most of which are clean and up to scratch. Young people may prefer to stay in Kreuzberg for its lively night scene.

rooms, a good standard of service and handily central location just off Kurfürstendamm. Facilities include a gym, a wellness zone and a couple of decent eateries.
⊞ D7 ⊠ Grolmanstrasse 41–3 ☎ 030 88 42 60
🚇 U-Bahn Uhlandstrasse

RESIDENZ BERLIN
www.hotel-residenz.com
Jugendstil architecture features in this 80-room hotel near Ku'damm. There is a restaurant too.
⊞ D7 ⊠ Meinekestrasse 9 ☎ 030 88 44 30 🚇 U-Bahn Kurfürstendamm

RIVERSIDE ROYAL HOTEL AND SPA
www.tolles-hotel.de
All the rooms in this small hotel on the banks of the River Spree have been individually designed and decorated with antique furnishings, mirrors and chandeliers. Some have a great view over the river.
⊞ J4 ⊠ Friedrichstrasse 105–106 ☎ 030 28 49 00 🚇 U- and S-Bahn Friedrichstrasse

TIERGARTEN BERLIN
www.hotel-tiergarten.de
Effortlessly combines the efficiency of a modern business hotel and more than a little of the charm of a privately owned lodging, in an early 1900s building with courtyard just north of the Spree.
⊞ F4 ⊠ Alt-Moabit 89 ☎ 030 39 98 96 🚇 U-Bahn Turmstrasse

Luxury Hotels

ESPLANADE GRAND HOTEL

www.esplanade.de
The last word in luxury and comfort, in rooms from large doubles all the way up to the stellar penthouse suite.
➕ G7 ✉ Lützowufer 15 ☎ 030 25 47 80 🚇 U-Bahn Nollendorfplatz

GRAND HYATT

www.berlin.grand.hyatt.com
This hotel has city views, 342 rooms, a swimming pool and fitness center. Some rooms have a view of the Tiergarten.
➕ H6 ✉ Marlene-Dietrich-Platz 2 ☎ 030 25 53 12 34 🚇 U- or S-Bahn Potsdamer Platz

HILTON BERLIN

www.hilton.de
In a great location, this hotel has 500 rooms, plus bars, restaurants, fitness area, pool and fabulous views over the Gendarmenmarkt.
➕ K6 ✉ Mohrenstrasse 30 ☎ 030 20 23 0 🚇 U-Bahn Hausvogteiplatz

HOTEL ADLON KEMPINSKI BERLIN

www.hotel-adlon.de
This historic 382-room hotel, at the Brandenburg Gate, is one of the city's most luxurious.
➕ J5 ✉ Unter den Linden 77 ☎ 030 226 10 🚇 S-Bahn Unter den Linden

HOTEL BRANDEN-BURGER HOF

www.brandenburger-hof.com
Stylish late 19th-century building, near the Kaiser Wilhelm Memorial Church. Winter garden restaurant, and 82 rooms.
➕ E7 ✉ Eislebener Strasse 14 ☎ 030 21 40 50 🚇 U-Bahn Augsburger Strasse

HOTEL DE ROME

www.hotelderome.com
Housed in a colonnaded, neoclassical former Dresdner Bank building (1899), this Rocco Forte hotel, which opened in 2006, is replete with modern design elegance.
➕ K5 ✉ Behrenstrasse 37 ☎ 030 460 60 90 🚇 U-Bahn Französische Strasse

THE SHOW GOES ON

The Hotel Adlon Kempinski Berlin bears a famous name, but it is not the original Hotel Adlon, which opened in 1907 and soon became a hangout for Europe's blue bloods. Between the wars, Hollywood stars and other celebrities kept the name in lights. The Adlon survived World War II only to succumb to a fire started by Russian troops celebrating victory in its wine cellar. The new Adlon opened in 1997 and has taken on much of the original's luster.

INTERCONTINENTAL BERLIN

www.berlin.intercontinental.com
The city's most glamorous hotel has 577 rooms, a swimming pool, sauna and a business facility.
➕ F6 ✉ Budapester Strasse 2 ☎ 030 260 20 🚇 U- or S-Bahn Zoologischer Garten

KEMPINSKI HOTEL BRISTOL BERLIN

www.kempinski.com
Chandeliers, deep carpets and courtous service are constant reminders of this hotel's resplendent past. There are 303 rooms, a fitness room and swimming pool.
➕ D7 ✉ Kurfürstendamm 27 ☎ 030 88 43 40 🚇 U-Bahn Uhlandstrasse

SAVOY BERLIN

www.hotel-savoy.com
This is an elegant hotel with a large roof terrace and many of the amenities of the city's top hotels, but with more user-friendly rates.
➕ D7 ✉ Fasanenstrasse 9–10 ☎ 030 31 10 30 🚇 U-Bahn Uhlandstrasse

SOFITEL BERLIN GENDARMENMARKT

www.sofitel.com
This hotel has dark marble and frosted glass in its classy rooms and guests can enjoy views of the Gendarmenmarkt.
➕ K5 ✉ Charlottenstrasse 50–52 ☎ 030 20 37 50 🚇 U-Bahn Französische Strasse

Use this section to help you in planning your visit to Berlin and getting around once you are there. You will also find useful tips and a section on language.

Need to Know

Planning Ahead

When to Go

Expect rain at any time. Summer can be hot and humid. April to June is the most comfortable period to visit. The arts scene is liveliest between October and May. From late November to Christmas the city is resplendent with decorations and the streets are filled with markets.

TIME

Berlin is one hour ahead of the UK, six hours ahead of New York, and nine hours ahead of Los Angeles.

AVERAGE DAILY MAXIMUM TEMPERATURES

JAN	FEB	MAR	APR	MAY	JUN	JUL	AUG	SEP	OCT	NOV	DEC
36°F	37°F	46°F	55°F	66°F	72°F	75°F	73°F	68°F	55°F	45°F	37°F
2°C	3°C	8°C	13°C	19°C	22°C	24°C	23°C	20°C	13°C	7°C	3°C

Spring (mid-March to May) is extremely pleasant, with flowers and trees coming into bloom throughout the parks and along the avenues.
Summer (June to early September) can be hot with the occasional dramatic thunder storm.
Fall (mid-September to November) is comfortable, but changeable with fine bright weather often preceded by periods of drizzle and grey skies.
Winter (December to mid-March) is extremely cold with occasional snowfalls, but it is common to experience crisp, bright days.

WHAT'S ON

On any given day, Berlin has around 250 exhibitions and more than 400 independent theater groups, 170 museums, 200 art galleries and 150 auditoriums. Check the listings magazines for details of events.

January *6-Day Race:* Cycling event at the Velodrom, Landsberger Allee.

February *International Film Festival (Berlinale):* The world's filmmakers come to Potsdamer Platz.

May *Karneval der Kulturen:* Carnival of Cultures, Kreuzberg.

Lange Nacht der Museen: More than 100 museums are open after midnight.

June *Fête de la Musique:* Concerts (from rock to classical) at Mitte, Friedrichshain, Prenzlauer Berg, Kreuzberg and other open-air venues.

Christopher Street Day: Gay and lesbian procession.

September *Musikfest:* Three weeks of classical music concerts at various venues around the city.

September/October *Berlin Marathon.*

October *German Unity Day* (3 Oct): Street festivals on Unter den Linden.

November *Jazz Festival Berlin:* For five days, jazz concerts are held citywide.

December *Christmas Markets:* All month at Opernpalais (Unter den Linden 5), Breitscheidplatz, Gendarmenmarkt, Winterfeldtplatz (Sunday only) and Spandau Altstadt.

New Year: Celebrations at the Brandenburg Gate and a gala evening at Staatsoper.

Useful Websites

www.visitberlin.de
The official site for the Berlin tourist board with details of hotels, sightseeing, guided tours and current events. You can order theater and concert tickets online and make hotel bookings from their list of approved hotels. Also in English.

www.berlin.de
The city of Berlin's official site with details of all the current events in both English and German.

www.berlinonline.de
A site providing information on life in the city with news, jobs, current events, clubbing, shopping and ticket information. In German only.

www.uberlin.co.uk
Quirky expat website packed with unusual listings, fashion, music and insider tips, all in English.

www.freshmilk.de
A creative site in German only dedicated to multimedia, modern art and culture.

www.tip-berlin.de
The official German-language site for the listings magazine *Tip*, detailing the major events and what is going on in the city in the way of films, music and partying in the month ahead.

www.zitty.de
In German only, the official site for the listings magazine *Zitty*, reviewing the top films, restaurants and bars in Berlin.

www.berlin-life.com
A locally produced online guide in English, with good what's-on and where-to-go information, and restaurant reviews.

www.bvg.de
Berlin public transportation site in English and German giving information on city travel.

PRIME TRAVEL SITES

www.fodors.com
A complete travel-planning site. You can research prices and weather; book air tickets, cars and rooms; ask questions (and get answers) from fellow travelers; and find links to other sites.

INTERNET CAFÉS

24hr Internetcafé am Adenauerpltz
➕ B7 ✉ Kurfürstendamm 161 ☎ 030 89 40 96 90
🕐 24/7 🚇 U-Bahn Adenauerplatz

PIPO-Internet-Telecafé
➕ K3 ✉ Torstrasse 22
☎ 030 28 09 67 30
🕐 10am–midnight
🚇 U-Bahn Oranienburger Tor

Surf and Sushi
➕ K4 ✉ Oranienburger Strasse 17 ☎ 030 28 38 48 98 🕐 Noon–late 🚇 S-Bahn Hackescher Markt

Getting There

For the latest passport and visa information, look up the embassy website at www.london.diplo.de. For latest information for visitors from the United States check the embassy website at www.germany.usembassy.gov

INSURANCE

EU nationals receive reduced-cost medical treatment with the EHIC card—obtain this card before traveling. Full health and travel insurance is still advised. US visitors should check their health coverage before departure and buy a supplementary policy as necessary.

AIRPORTS

Berlin is currently served by two airports: Tegel, to the northwest, and Schönefeld, to the southeast. The Schönefeld site is being expanded into a new airport, Berlin Brandenburg International, which is due to replace the existing airports in 2015.

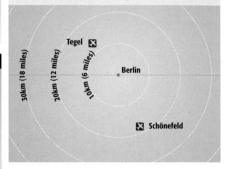

ARRIVING AT TEGEL AIRPORT

Off map to northwest. For airport information ☎ 030 60 91 11 50. The airport is linked to the city via the bus network. Bus 109 from the airport will take you to Zoologischer Garten Station, as does bus X9. Bus 128 goes to the north of Berlin, while the TXL bus goes to Alexanderplatz, and then beyond to Prenzlauer Berg. A taxi right into the city costs about €15 and takes around 20 minutes. For more information, see www.berlin-airport.de.

ARRIVING AT SCHÖNEFELD AIRPORT

Off map to southeast. For airport information ☎ 030 60 91 11 50. There is a free shuttle transfer from the terminal building to Berlin-Schönefeld airport station. The Airport Express takes passengers from the airport to Berlin's main rail station (Hauptbahnhof 28) and there are also S-Bahn and RegionalBahn trains. Buses X7 and 171 link the terminal building with the Rudow U-Bahn station. A taxi to the city costs about €25 and takes around 40 minutes. For more information about arriving at the airport, see www.berlin-airport.de.

BERLIN BRANDENBURG INTERNATIONAL

The new high-tech airport being built at Schönefeld, 20km (12 miles) from Berlin city centre, is due to be completed in 2015. It will have direct motorway access and a six-track rail station connecting directly into central Berlin and the surrounding region, and will handle all the region's air traffic; Tegel will close. For more information, see www.berlin-airport.de.

ARRIVING BY BUS

The central bus station (Zentraler Omnibusbahnhof/ZOB ☎ 030 302 53 61; www.iob-berlin.de) is on Masurenallee, opposite the International Conference Centre (ICC), in the district of Charlottenburg.

ARRIVING BY TRAIN

There are good connections from major European cities. The city's main station for international and long-distance services is Berlin Hauptbahnhof. Other city stations handle regional and local services. For train information: Deutsche Bahn (German Railways) ✚ D6 ✉ Hardenbergplatz 11 ☎ 11 8 61 (24 hour), www.db.de.

ARRIVING BY CAR

The A10/E55 ring road provides access to Berlin from the north, south, east and west. If you intend to bring your car into central Berlin, it is a good idea to find a hotel with parking (preferably in advance) as there are few car parks and little on-street parking in and around the city.

CUSTOMS

Visiting from another EU country:

3,200 cigarettes or 400 cigarillos or 200 cigars or 3kg of smoking tobacco.

10 liters of spirits or 20 liters of fortified wine (such as port or sherry) or 90 liters of wine (of which only 60 liters can be sparkling wine) or 110 liters of beer.

Visiting Germany from outside the EU:

200 cigarettes or 100 cigarillos or 50 cigars or 250g of smoking tobacco.

1 liter of spirits or strong liqueurs.

2 liters of still table wine or 2 liters of fortified wine, sparkling wine or other liqueurs.

50cc perfume.

250cc/ml of eau de toilette.

Getting Around

POTSDAM BOUND

To do a side trip to historic Potsdam (▷ 104–105), the quickest way to get there under your own steam from the city is to take S-Bahn line S1. It passes through the heart of Berlin and you can catch it at stops that include Hackescher Markt, Unter den Linden and Potsdamer Platz.

VISITORS WITH DISABILITIES

Berlin has a wheelchair breakdown service, Der Rollstuhlpannendienst, that can be called out around the clock and will come out to fix any problems on the spot like the AA or AAA break-down service
☎ 0177 83 35 773, www.rollstuhlpannendienst.de

Buses have rear-door access and safety straps for wheelchairs.

Berlin has an excellent public transport network, with two urban rail services and bus and tram routes. The local transport authority is the Berliner Verkehrsbetriebe (BVG).

● BVG Information Service. Timetables and tickets ☎ 030 194 49; www.bvg.de
● S-Bahn Berlin GmbH Information Service www.s-bahn-berlin.de

TYPES OF TICKET

● The 24-hour ticket (*Tageskarte*) and the weekly *7-Tage-Karte* allow unlimited travel on the BVG network (trains, buses, trams and the ferry from Wannsee to Kladow). The weekly ticket covers unlimited travel during any seven-day period from validation until midnight on the seventh day.
● A single one-way ticket (*Einzelfahrausweis*) is valid for two hours. You can transfer or interrupt your travel.
● The *Kurzstrecke* (short-distance ticket) is valid on the U- and S-Bahn for up to three stops including transfers, or for six stops only (bus/tram).
● BerlinWelcomeCard entitles one adult and up to three children age 6–14 to free BVG travel for two, three or five days as well as reductions on sightseeing trips, museums and theaters. Ask at your hotel, tourist information offices or U-Bahn ticket offices.
● Children under 14: reduced-rate travel; children under 6: free.

THE METRO

● The U-Bahn (underground railway) and S-Bahn (city railway) are interchangeable.
● You must buy a ticket from station foyers or from vending machines on platforms. Validate your ticket at a machine on the platform before boarding the train. Routes are referred to by the final stop on the line.
● Trains run every 5 or 10 minutes, Mon–Fri 5am–midnight; Sat–Sun (approximately) 4am–2am. On Friday and Saturday there is a 24-hour service on several city trains and

underground lines that runs every 15 minutes.
● You may take bicycles on the U-Bahn on
weekdays between 9am and 2pm and after
5.30pm, and all weekend. Cyclists may travel
on the S-Bahn at any time. You will need to buy
a bicycle ticket.

BUSES

● Central Bus Station, Funkturm ☎ 030 30 10
01 75; www.iob-berlin.de
● Enter double-decker buses at the front and
leave by the doors in the middle or at the back.
Pay the driver with small change or show your
ticket (see above). Multiple tickets, also valid
for U- and S-Bahn, can be bought from vending
machines at some bus stops or at U-Bahn stations, but not from the driver.
● Routes 100 and 200 are particularly useful,
departing from Zoologischer Garten Station
every 10 minutes and linking the West End with
Unter den Linden and Alexanderplatz.
● More than 70 night buses operate half-hourly
from 1am to 4am. Line N19 runs through the
city every 15 minutes.

STRASSENBAHNEN (TRAMS)

● Trams operate largely in eastern Berlin. Tickets
are available from vending machines inside the
trams.

MAPS AND TIMETABLES

● Obtain timetables and maps from large
U-Bahn ticket offices such as Alexanderplatz
☎ 030 194 49; www.bvg.de.

TAXIS

● Taxis are good value, with stands throughout
the city. Only use cabs with a meter.
● There is a small surcharge for baggage.
● Not all drivers know their way, so travel with
your own map.
● Central taxi phone numbers ☎ 030 44 33
222 or 0800 222 22 55
● Chauffeur service ☎ 030 456 11 11
● Bike taxis (velotaxis) ☎ 030 4400 56 20

BVG FERRIES

BVG ferry lines in the
Wannsee and Köpenick
areas include services
from Wannsee to Kladow,
Glienicker Bridge to Sacrow,
Grünau to Wendenschloss
and around the Müggelsee.

CAR SHARING

Visitors can telephone a
Mitfahrzentrale (ride center)
to arrange a lift to other
German cities in a private car
(rates to be agreed before-
hand). The Mitfahrzentrale is
located at:
U-Bahn Zoologischer Garten,
platform 2 ➕ D6 ☎ 030
194 40 (Mon–Fri 9–8, Sat–
Sun 10–6)

Essential Facts

● United Kingdom
✉ Wilhelmstrasse 70–71
☎ 030 20 45 70
● United States ✉ Pariser
Platz 2 ☎ 030 238 51 74

EUROS

The euro is the official currency of Germany. Bank notes come in denominations of 5, 10, 20, 50, 100, 200 and 500 euros; and coins in denominations of 1, 2, 5, 10, 20 and 50 cents and 1 and 2 euros.

CUSTOMS REGULATIONS

For details of duty-free allowances for visitors from within the EU and from countries outside the EU, see list given in the "Customs" panel on page 117.

ELECTRICITY

● 230 volts on a two-pin plug.

LOST PROPERTY

● Police, Tempelhof ✚ Off map to southeast ✉ Platz der Luftbrücke 6 ☎ 030 75 60 31 01
● BVG Transport Lost and Found (Fündburo)
✚ G8 ✉ Potsdamer Strasse 180–182
☎ 030 19 44 9

MEDICINES

● Take any specially prescribed medications with you. Check on the generic name of any drugs before you leave home, in case you need to replace your prescription while away.

MEDICAL AND DENTAL TREATMENT

● There are plenty of English-speaking doctors in Berlin. For a referral service telephone the medical emergency number.
● Emergency numbers (within Berlin):
Medical ☎ 01804. Dental ☎ 22 55 23 62
● EU citizens receive free health care (excluding dental care) on production of their EHIC card, but private medical insurance is still advised and is essential for all other visitors.

MONEY MATTERS

● Exchange offices (*Wechselstuben*) can be found all over Berlin: Hauptbahnhof (main station) ✚ H4 ⊙ Daily 7.30am–10pm; Friedrichstrasse station ✚ J5 ⊙ Mon–Fri 7am–8pm, Sat–Sun 8–8.
● Automatic cash dispensers (ATMs) can be found citywide.
● Most major credit cards are recognized but not widely accepted.
● Euro traveler's checks are preferred, but those in US dollars are acceptable.

OPENING HOURS

● **Shops** Mon–Fri 9.30–8, Sat 10–8. These are typical opening hours; some shops may open 24 hours.

● **Banks** Mon–Fri 9.30–3. Afternoons vary.

● **Pharmacies** Mon–Fri 9.30–6.30, Sat 9–2 ☎ 030 31 00 31 for night pharmacies.

STUDENT VISITORS

● Discounts on public transport, in museums and some theaters are available with an International Student Identity Card.

● European youth passes are also available for people under 26.

SENSIBLE PRECAUTIONS

● Although Berlin is one of the safer European cities, always remain on your guard. Keep a close eye on bags and do not hang them on the back of chairs in restaurants.

● Avoid poorly lighted areas. Some places such as Motzstrasse can become seedy red-light districts at night.

● Keep wallets and purses concealed when travelling on the U-Bahn and trams.

TELEPHONES

● In phone boxes marked Kartentelefon use phone cards, available from post offices, petrol stations and newspaper kiosks.

● Boxes marked "International" and telephones in post offices are for long-distance calls.

● Calls are cheapest after 10pm at night and on Sunday.

● Follow the dialling instructions (in several languages) in the box.

● To call the UK from Berlin dial 0044, then omit the first 0 from the area code.

● To call Berlin from the UK dial 0049 30, then the number.

● To call the US from Berlin dial 001.

● To call Berlin from the US dial 01149 30, then the number.

● For local information: 11833; for international information: 11834

EMERGENCY PHONE NUMBERS

● Coins are not needed for emergency calls from public telephones: Police ☎ 110; Fire and Ambulance ☎ 112

● American Hotline: crisis hotline and free, recorded medical referral service ☎ 0177 8141510

SIGHTSEEING TOURS

BBS Berliner Bären Stadtrundfahrt
Daily tours and days out in eight languages. Departures from Ku'damm and Alexanderplatz. ☎ 030 35 19 52 70

Berolina Stadtrundfahrten
Daily bus tours of Berlin and Potsdam–Sanssouci in eight languages. Departures from Ku'damm at Meinekestrasse ☎ 030 88 56 80 30

Berlin by boat
Starting from close to the Berliner Dom, you can take a boat tour along the River Spree through "historical Berlin" ☎ 030 53 63 600; www.sternundkreis.de
Daily; tours last one hour

PUBLIC HOLIDAYS

● 1 January; Good Friday; Easter Monday; 1 May; Ascension Day; Pentecost Monday; 3 October (German Unity Day); Christmas Day; 26 December.

POST OFFICES

● ✉ Alte Potsdamer Strasse 7 🕔 Mon–Fri 6am–9pm, Sat 7am–9pm, Sun 11am–7pm ✉ Friederichstrasse 69 🕔 Mon–Fri 9.30am–7pm, Sat 9.30am–2pm
● Stamps can be bought from vending machines on Ku'damm, as well as from post offices.
● Postboxes are bright yellow.

TOILETS

● Men's toilets are labelled *Herren*, women's *Damen* or *Frauen*.
● Public toilets, run by private company Wall, can be found all over the city. You have to pay to use them, but they are clean and well kept.

TOURIST INFORMATION OFFICES

● Berlin Tourismus Marketing (head office) ✉ Am Karlsbad 11 ☎ 030 25 00 25; www.visitberlin.de
● Berlin Hauptbahnhof (main rail station) 🚏 H4 ✉ Ground Floor, North Entrance, Europlatz 1 🕔 Daily 8am–10pm 🚇 U- or S-Bahn Hauptbahnhof
● Neues Kranzler Eck Passage 🚏 D7 ✉ Kurfürstendamm 22 🕔 Mon–Sat 9.30am–8pm 🚇 U-Bahn Kurfürstendamm
● Brandenburger Tor 🚏 J5 ✉ South Wing, Pariser Platz 🕔 Apr–Oct daily 9.30am 7pm; Nov–Mar 9.30am–6pm 🚇 U- or S-Bahn Brandenburger Tor
● Fernsehturm 🚏 L5 ✉ Panoramastrasse 1a 🕔 Apr–Oct daily 10am–6pm; Nov–Mar daily 10am–4pm 🚇 U- or S-Bahn Alexanderplatz

WOMEN TRAVELERS

● Schokofabrik (Women's Centre): 🚏 Off map to southeast ✉ Marianenstrasse 6 ☎ 030 615 29 99 🍴 Café

PLACES OF WORSHIP

Protestant	Berliner Dom (▷ 77) 🚏 L5 ☎ 030 20 26 91 11 🕔 Services Sun 10am, 6pm (Evensong in English Thu 6pm)
Roman Catholic	Hedwigskirche (▷ 68) 🚏 K5 ☎ 030 203 48 10 🕔 Mass Sun 8am, 10am, 12, 6pm, Sat 7pm
Anglican/Episcopal	St George's 🚏 Off map to west ✉ Preussenallee 17–19 🕔 Morning service Sun 10am. Holy Communion Sun 8am
Liberal Jewish	Synagogue Pestalozzistrasse 🚏 C6 ✉ Pestalozzistrasse 12–14 ☎ 030 313 84 11 🕔 Services Fri 7pm, Sat 9.30am
Orthodox Jewish	Adass Jisroel 🚏 K4 ✉ Tucholskystrasse 40 ☎ 030 304 12 80 🕔 Services Fri 5pm; Sat 9.30am
Moslem	Sehitlik Mosque 🚏 Off map, south of M9 ✉ Columbiadamm 128 ☎ 030 692 11 18 🕔 Open daily

Language

BASICS

ja	yes
nein	no
bitte	please
danke	thank you
guten Morgen	good morning
guten Abend	good evening
gute Nacht	good night
auf Wiedersehen	goodbye
heute	today
gestern	yesterday
morgen	tomorrow
die Speisekarte	menu
das Frühstück	breakfast
das Mittagessen	lunch
das Abendessen	dinner
der Weisswein	white wine
der Rotwein	red wine
das Bier	beer
das Brot	bread
die Milch	milk
der Zucker	sugar
das Wasser	water
die Rechnung	bill
das Zimmer	room
offen	open
geschlossen	closed
wieviel?	how much?
teuer	expensive
billig	cheap
sprechen Sie Englisch?	do you speak English?
Ich spreche kein Deutsch	I don't speak German
Ich verstehe nicht	I don't understand
Entschuldigen Sie	Excuse me
der Bahnhof	train station
der Flughafen	airport
die Bank	bank
das Postamt	post office
die Polizei	police
das Krankenhaus	hospital

USEFUL WORDS

klein	small
gross	large
schnell	quickly
kalt	cold
warm	hot
gut	good

123

Timeline

A BERLIN FIRST

Werner Siemens and Johann Georg Malske manufactured the first telegraph in a house on Schöneberger Strasse.

THE WALL

In 1961, 200,000 people escaped the GDR in the East and fled to the West, 152,000 of them via Berlin. On the night of 12 August 1961 the GDR closed the border, erecting a wall of barbed wire, concrete slabs and stones to halt the flow of refugees. This was followed by the building of the Wall, a concrete structure 12km (7.5 miles) long. The border was heavily guarded and during the time the Wall stood 152 people lost their lives trying to escape.

Left to right: Frederick the Great; detail of the crest of the German Unification flag; Hitler enters the Sudetenland, 1938; WW II commemorative plaques at the 1936 Olympic Stadium; signs at former Checkpoint Charlie; entrance to the 1936 Olympic Stadium

1244 First recorded mention of Berlin.

1359 Berlin becomes a member of the Hanseatic League trading association.

1443 Frederick II of Brandenburg builds the first Berlin castle (Schloss).

1448 Berliners defend their privileges in the "Berliner Unwille" revolt.

1618–48 Berlin is devastated by Austrian and Swedish armies during the Thirty Years' War. The population is halved to less than 6,000.

1701 Elector Frederick III proclaims himself King Frederick I of Prussia. In 1740 Frederick the Great becomes king.

1806 Napoleon enters Berlin.

1848 Germany's "bourgeois revolution" sees demands for greater middle-class representation in government. Workers take to the barricades.

1871 Berlin becomes the capital of a united German Empire under Kaiser Wilhelm I and the Prime Minister of Prussia, Prince Otto von Bismarck.

1918 After the end of World War I, Kaiser Wilhelm II abdicates to make way for a German Republic.

1920s Despite growing social and economic instability, Berlin becomes a cultural powerhouse. Grosz, Einstein, Brecht and Gropius flourish.

1933 Hitler becomes German Chancellor.

1936 Berlin hosts the Olympic Games.

1938 On the "night of breaking glass" the Nazis orchestrate the destruction of Jewish properties and synagogues.

1939–45 World War II.

1945 Berlin lies in ruins, its population reduced from 4 million to 2.8 million.

1945–89 A city divided (▷ side panel).

1989 On 9 November the collapse of communism in Eastern Europe leads to the opening of the Berlin Wall and its eventual demise.

1990 Germany is unified.

2000 Berlin once again becomes the capital of a united Germany.

2006 The Olympiastadion hosts the soccer world cup final.

2014 The 25th anniversary of the fall of the Berlin Wall marked with celebrations and fireworks.

A CITY DIVIDED

1945 Berlin is divided into four zones of occupation, administered by French, British, US and Soviet forces.
1948–49 A Soviet attempt to force the Western Allies to withdraw from Berlin by blockading the city is foiled by a gigantic airlift of supplies.
1949 Germany is divided into the Federal Republic and the communist German Democratic Republic. Berlin is stranded in the GDR.
1953 Construction workers in East Berlin, protesting at low wages, provoke a full-scale uprising, which is put down by Soviet tanks.
1961 The flood of East Germans to the West is staunched by the building of the Berlin Wall.
1963 John F. Kennedy demonstrates American support for West Berlin in his famous "Ich bin ein Berliner" speech.

Index

Published by AA Publishing, a trading name of AA Media Limited, whose registered office is Fanum House, Basing View, Basingstoke, Hampshire RG21 4EA. Registered number 06112600.

© AA Media Limited 2016
First published 2005
New edition 2016

WRITTEN BY Christopher and Melanie Rice
ADDITIONAL WRITING BY George McDonald
UPDATED BY Marc di Duca
SERIES EDITOR Clare Ashton
DESIGN WORK Tracey Freestone, Nick Johnston
IMAGE RETOUCHING AND REPRO Ian Little

Colour separation by AA Digital Department
Printed and bound by Leo Paper Products, China

A CIP catalogue record for this book is available from the British Library.

ISBN 978-0-7495-7738-4

We have tried to ensure accuracy in this guide, but things do change, so please let us know if you have any comments at travelguides@theAA.com.

A05378
Maps in this title produced from mapping © MAIRDUMONT / Falk Verlag 2014
Transport map © Communicarta Ltd, UK

The Automobile Association would like to thank the following photographers, companies and picture libraries for their assistance in the preparation of this book.

2-18t AA/Doug Traverso; 4l AA/Tony Souter; 5c/b AA/Simon McBride; 6cl AA/Simon McBride; 6cc AA/Jonathan Smith; 6cr AA/Simon McBride; 6bl AA/Simon McBride; 6br AA/Clive Sawyer; 7cl AA/Simon McBride; 7cc AA/Jonathan Smith; 7cr AA/Clive Sawyer; 7bl AA/Clive Sawyer; 7bc AA/Clive Sawyer; 7br AA/Jonathan Smith; 10ctr AA/Simon McBride; 10cr Photodisc; 10cbr AA/Tony Souter; 10/11b AA/Tony Souter; 11ctl AA/Tony Souter; 11cl AA/Simon McBride; 11cbl AA/Tony Souter; 12b AA Photodisc; 13ctl AA/Simon McBride; 13cl AA/Clive Sawyer; 13cbl AA/Simon McBride; 13bl AA/Tony Souter; 14ctr AA/Jonathan Smith; 14cr AA/Jonathan Smith; 14cbr AA/Simon McBride; 14br AA/Jonathan Smith; 15b AA/Tony Souter; 16ctr AA/Jonathan Smith; 16cbr AA/Simon McBride; 16br AA/James Tims; 17ctl AA/Clive Sawyer; 17cl AA Digitalvision; 17cbl AA/Jonathan Smith; 17bl AA/Jonathan Smith; 18ctr AA Image 100; 18cr AA/Tony Souter; 18cbr AA/Tony Souter; 18br AA/Clive Sawyer; 19a (top down) AA/Clive Sawyer; 19b AA/Simon McBride; 19c AA/Jonathan Smith; 19d AA/Adrian Baker; 19e AA/Jonathan Smith; 19f AA/Jonathan Smith; 19g AA/Adrian Baker; 19h AA/Simon McBride; 20/21 AA/Simon McBride; 24 AA/Clive Sawyer; 25t AA/Jonathan Smith; 25cl AA/Tony Souter; 25cr AA/Tony Souter; 26t AA/Jonathan Smith; 26bl AA/Tony Souter; 26br AA/Jonathan Smith; 27t AA/Tony Souter; 27c AA/Tony Souter; 28 AA/Simon McBride; 29 AA/Simon McBride; 32l AA/Doug Traverso; 32r AA/Tony Souter; 33l AA/Simon McBride; 33r AA/Simon McBride; 34l EPA PHOTO/DPA/TIM BRAKEMEIER; 34r AA/Tony Souter; 35 AA/Adrian Baker; 36 AA Photodisc; 37 AA/Jonathan Smith; 38 AA/Jonathan Smith; 39 AA/Jonathan Smith; 42tl AA/Jonathan Smith; 42-43t AA/Jonathan Smith; 42cl AA/Jonathan Smith; 42cr AA/Jonathan Smith; 43cl AA/Jonathan Smith; 43r AA/Jonathan Smith; 44l Courtesy of Bauhaus-archive; 44r Courtesy of Bauhaus-archive; 45t AA/Jonathan Smith; 45b Filmmuseum Berlin/Hans Scherhaufer; 46 AA/Adrian Baker; 47t AA/Michelle Chaplow; 47c AA Digitalvision; 48 AA/Tony Souter; 49 AA/Simon McBride; 52 Guy Moberly/Alamy; 53 Silke Reents; 54t AA/Jonathan Smith; 54bl AA/Adrian Baker; 54br AA/Adrian Baker; 55t AA Photodisc; 55c AA Photodisc; 56 AA/Tony Souter; 57 AA/Jonathan Smith; 60l AA/Tony Souter; 60r AA/Clive Sawyer; 61l AA/Tony Souter; 61c AA/Tony Souter; 61r AA/Simon McBride; 62 AA/Clive Sawyer; 62/63 AA/Clive Sawyer; 64l AA/Jonathan Smith; 64c AA/Clive Sawyer; 64r AA/Clive Sawyer; 65l AA/Simon McBride; 65r AA/Simon McBride; 66l AA/Jonathan Smith; 66-67t AA/Simon McBride; 66cr AA/Tony Souter; 67l AA/Jonathan Smith; 67r AA/Jonathan Smith; 68l AA/Simon McBride; 68r AA/Tony Souter; 69t AA/Jonathan Smith; 69bl AA/Simon McBride; 69br AA/A Kouprianoff; 70 AA/Paul Kenward; 71 AA Brand X Pics; 72 AA/Clive Sawyer; 73 AA/Tony Souter; 76l AA/Simon McBride; 76c AA/Jonathan Smith; 76r AA/Jonathan Smith; 77l AA/Clive Sawyer; 77r AA/Simon McBride; 78l AA/Simon McBride; 78cr AA/Tony Souter; 78/79t AA/Simon McBride; 79tr AA/Tony Souter; 79cl AA/Adrian Baker; 79cr AA/Simon McBride; 80l AA/Clive Sawyer; 80r AA/Clive Sawyer; 81l AA/Simon McBride; 81c AA/Jonathan Smith; 81r AA/Simon McBride; 82-83t AA/Jonathan Smith; 82bl AA/Clive Sawyer; 82br AA/Tony Souter; 83bl AA/Adrian Baker; 83br AA/Clive Sawyer; 84 AA/Adrian Baker; 85t AA/Simon McBride; 85c Brand X Pics; 86 AA/Eric Meacher; 87 AA/Tony Souter; 90 Silke Reents; 91l AA/Clive Sawyer; 91r © Eric Nathan/Alamy; 92t AA/Jonathan Smith; 92b Silke Reents; 93t AA/Clive Sawyer; 93c Photodisc; 94 AA/Clive Sawyer; 95 AA/Jonathan Smith; 98l AA/Tony Souter; 98r AA/Tony Souter; 99 AA/Tony Souter; 100l AA/Clive Sawyer; 100r AA/Adrian Baker; 101-103t AA/Jonathan Smith; 101bl AA/Adrian Baker; 101br AA/Simon McBride; 102bl Andreas_T_Feuer; 102br AA/Clive Sawyer; 103b Silke Reents; 104-105t AA/Simon McBride; 104b AA/Jonathan Smith; 105b AA/Simon McBride; 106t AA/Jonathan Smith; 106b AA/Tony Souter; 107 AA/Jonathan Smith; 108-112t AA/Clive Sawyer; 108ctr AA/Jonathan Smith; 108cr AA/Jonathan Smith; 108cbr AA/Pete Bennett; 108br AA/Jonathan Smith; 113 AA/Jonathan Smith; 114-125t AA/Simon McBride; 117b AA/Simon McBride; 118b AA/Tony Souter; 119b AA/Tony Souter; 121b AA/Tony Souter; 123c AA/Max Jourdan; 123b AA/Jonathan Smith; 124bl AA; 124bc AA/Doug Traverso; 124br Illustrated London News; 125bl AA/Adrian Baker; 125bc AA/Tony Souter; 125br AA/Adrian Baker;

Every effort has been made to trace the copyright holders, and we apologize in advance for any accidental errors. We would be happy to apply the corrections in the following edition of this publication.

Titles in the Series